Seaside Gardening

REVISED AND EXPANDED

Seaside Gardening

Theodore James, Jr., and Harry Haralambou ❦ Photographs by Harry Haralambou

Abrams, New York

REVISED AND EXPANDED

For Cathy Zgaljic

Page 1: *Lythrum salicaria* 'Morden's Pink' and hydrangea
Pages 2–3: Clumps of grasses and a moon-gate with climbing rose 'Aloha'
Left: Privet
Opposite above: Daylilies
Opposite center: Sedum and ferns
Opposite below: Bayberry

Editors: Eric Himmel, Sharon AvRutick
Designers: Darilyn Lowe Carnes, Shawn Dahl
Production Manager: Jane Searle

Library of Congress Cataloging-in-Publication Data

James, Theodore.
  Seaside gardening / by Theodore James, Jr., and Harry Haralambou ; photographs by Harry Haralambou.—2nd ed.
    p. cm.
  Includes bibliographical references and index.
  ISBN 0–8109–5517–2 (hardcover : alk. paper)
1. Seaside gardening. 2. Seaside gardening—Atlantic Coast (U.S.)
I. Haralambou, Harry. II. Title.

SB460.J36 2006
635.9'0914'6–dc22

2005022193

Printed and bound in China
10 9 8 7 6 5 4 3 2 1

harry n. abrams, inc.
a subsidiary of La Martinière Groupe

115 West 18th Street
New York, NY 10011
www.hnabooks.com

Contents

Introduction

Seaside Gardening is intended, above all, to be as useful as it is beautiful, and so it limits its scope to the temperate regions of eastern North America from southern Canada south to North Carolina, an area with a climate similar to Northern Europe's and somewhat colder winters than the Pacific Northwest. Gardening is an art that is intensely influenced by nature, and no one book could possibly offer adequate guidance to coastal gardeners everywhere. The subtropical areas of Florida and Southern California can host plants that are too tender to be grown in the rest of the country (not for us are the palms of Palm Beach). On the other hand, the climate there cannot support many of the hardy plants that are the staples of the northern gardener. Even the warmer temperate zones, such as the southern East Coast and the Pacific coast of Oregon and Washington, offer many species that would not survive farther north. Where climate is not a barrier, plants still may not travel far: an East Coast gardener could go a lifetime without setting eyes on the beach pine (*Pinus contorta*), a ubiquitous native of West Coast dunes and bogs from Mexico to Alaska.

To be able to show a range of seaside gardens, we chose to concentrate on three areas of the Northeast coast: the sandy beaches, wetlands, and rocky Long Island Sound shore of the east end of Long Island; the New Jersey shore, where seaside gardening can be most challenging; and the rockbound coast of central Maine. For many generations, gardening has been taken very seriously in these areas (the first Long Island nursery opened in 1737), and years of experience have left their mark on local gardeners. Long Island, with a seacoast and native flora that is in many ways typical of the lands that stretch north and south of it from Massachusetts to the Chesapeake, has always been and continues to be a focal point for innovative garden design, not only by gardeners, many of them artists, but by landscape designers and landscape architects who were employed by wealthy and sophisticated summer residents. Mt. Desert Island in Maine, where the coastal topography is quite different, has an equally splendid garden heritage, for some of the same reasons.

The seashore offers a very special atmosphere. Under skies that seem bluer and clearer than those farther inland, hot colors are hotter and cool colors are cooler. A seaside garden shrouded in mist and fog has a distinct aura of mystery. Storm clouds may bring an ambience of surreal calm. Prevailing winds will toss its leaves like waves in the sea. The evening light is often spectacular, bathing plantings in a shimmering iridescence, while crisp, clear mornings bring out the magnificent greens of nature. The invigorating salt air restores the spirit.

It is no wonder that so many residents of seaside areas turn to gardening as a primary pastime. Dropping the formality of city and suburban living, we get into our old garden clothes and relish the healthy exercise and rejuvenating, near spiritual, experience of gardening. There is nothing like a seaside garden to instruct us in the humbling wisdom that we are just one very small part of the entire scheme of God's earth.

In planning a garden, common sense is one guideline, and beyond that, experience—either one's own or that of seasoned gardeners—is a great teacher. Most seaside gardeners have to contend with drought conditions during the hot days of summer: they are given sandy soil that drains quickly and prevailing winds that dry out plantings, and they soon learn to adapt and to bend to the will of nature by

Native marsh mallows and reeds, both wetland plants,
flourish around a Long Island pond.

using plants that do not need constant watering. Along the rocky coast of Maine, gardeners utilize the small pockets of earth in rock crevices for plants that thrive in thin soil. On Long Island traditional shade trees, most of which do not do well near the ocean, have been supplanted by smaller trees that do.

Sooner or later, seaside gardeners learn to take advantage of the sea's gifts. For example, they use silver-foliaged plants to create contrast in texture and color. Almost without exception, these plants, which originated in seashore areas, add stunning beauty to a planting. Their pale greens seem cool in the harsh midday sun. Many gardeners go further and use flowers in cool colors—purples and blues with pinks. Others prefer summery, cheerful reds, yellows, and oranges. All have absorbed the hard lesson that a gardenesque look can be achieved by focusing on a few tried-and-true varieties.

Many seaside gardeners achieve stunning effects by including annuals in their plantings. These are generally pest and disease resistant, and more to the point, many are drought tolerant and thrive in the hot sun. And, since they live for only one year, it is not necessary to protect them from winter's cold. Each year, growers, recognizing the demand for these plants, are offering more and more unusual varieties of seedlings. These days, gardeners are also encouraged to try native plants, which are naturally adapted to seaside conditions. Tough, graceful grasses, both natives and garden hybrids, are being used more and more in the place of traditional shrubs and herbaceous perennial plants to create structure in gardens.

My personal preference is for the "cool" garden. Except in spring plantings and in the early blooming rock garden, where vibrant color sparks the landscape, I rarely use plants with orange, bright red, or sulfur-yellow blooms, favoring the blue-purple-pink spectrum with white and pale yellow for accents. I also like plants with silver- and blue-toned foliage. This is the color combination that the English garden designer and writer Gertrude Jekyll used. In this, I suppose, I declare my kinship to Maine gardeners rather than to my fellow gardeners on Long Island, for the gardens of Maine surveyed in this book owe much to the American landscape designer Beatrix Farrand, who had a famous garden on Mt. Desert Island and was influential in popularizing Jekyll's taste in America. After looking at the photographs of gardens designed by Tish Rehill, whose color sense is far more adventurous than my own, you may decide that I lack imagination, but I rarely have to worry about colors clashing and can concentrate on foliage, texture, autumn color, and other aspects of the plants. I love deep purple heliotrope with annual dusty miller or perennial lamb's ears. I am not charmed by hot-red annual salvia; screaming yellow, orange, or gold marigolds; or the shocking electric blue annual lobelia. I am quite taken with old-fashioned single hollyhocks.

You will undoubtedly find, as I have, that your taste in plants and color schemes will evolve with the years. I have all but phased out my temperamental modern roses, favoring the new English roses and the old garden varieties. Because heavy spring rain wreaks havoc with stately, tall German irises and blowsy double-pompon peonies, I now prefer shorter-growing irises and have acquired many lovely single peonies. None of these need staking, and they are considerably less flamboyant. As the garden has grown and grown, I have learned to make things easier for myself by growing plants that are better adapted to their environment.

And in the course of researching and experimenting with tropical plants and tender perennials for the second edition of this book, I have come to appreciate their vibrant colors and their potential for whimsy in the garden. Even I—a stick in the mud—can change.

In the pages that follow, you will find many beautiful photographs of exceptional gardens that we visited while gathering material for this book. You are bound to find ideas in them that you can adapt to your

The author's Peconic, New York, rock garden in May, designed with large sweeps of color. By late February, species crocus, Iris danfordiae, Iris reticulata, *snowdrops, and winter aconite are all in bloom.*

own property. Readers who do not have long experience gardening by the sea will find the Practical Guide, a chapter devoted to horticultural and practical advice, especially useful. Finally, there is an extensive plant list—the Plant Encyclopedic—designed to help you select plants for your own seaside garden.

In this second edition, we have added dozens of pictures and completely revised and updated the Encyclopedic, augmenting it with a lengthy section on tropicals and tender perennials (with a special emphasis on containers). We have also included many lists of newly available cultivars for you to explore.

The Water's Edge

Two chairs on the lawn make a garden. In this case, the lawn consists of graceful native American beach grass, one of the few plants that will thrive in the sand directly on the ocean. It must be said that there are conservationists who would disapprove of any recreational use of the primary dune, that is, the first dune on the beach that protects low-lying inland areas from the fury of the sea.

An ambitious planting on a sandy bluff above the ocean on the east end of Long Island includes various perennials and annuals partly shielded from the wind by a hillock of roses, which shelters a small pine. The garden, by designer Mary Beth Lee, includes dahlias, perennial phlox, chives, and, on the ocean side of the pool, a clump of zebra grass, and blends in with the native flora of the dune. Looking toward the east, in a photograph taken at dawn (opposite above), we see sedum (also above), fescue grass, Dahlberg daisies, and Swan River daisies. The perennial plantings are as permanent as nature permits this close to the ocean, while the annuals are added each spring.

This garden designed by Lisa Stamm and Dale Booher for a large house in Sagaponack, Long Island, is virtually surrounded by water. A stroll over the bridge takes one to the beach, while a few steps to the right, past a swimming pool, is a small estuary. The handsome planting comes as a surprise this close to the ocean, but none of the varieties is particularly difficult to grow: included are maiden grass (*Miscanthus sinensis* 'Gracillimus') and dwarf fountain grass (*Pennisetum alopecuroides* 'Hameln'), black-eyed Susan, Russian sage, purple loosestrife, sedum, and annual *Verbena* 'Sissinghurst.' The small trees that provide an extra measure of wind protection behind the border are Russian olives.

15

The late artist Mabel d'Amico's Amagansett, New York, property looks out over the dunes to an inlet of Peconic Bay. A lovely planting of lavender, lilies, and candytuft protected by a hillock of ivy and Virginia creeper blends gracefully into the landscape, as do the clumps of daylilies beyond. Her studio window holds a sea of colored glass bottles, in colors that seem uncannily in tune with the plantings outside.

16

On the bank of a small estuary of Peconic
Bay in Wainscott, New York, daffodils are
welcome under the dreary skies of early
spring. Among spring bulbs, daffodils are
well suited to seaside environments, since
they require little care, returning in profusion year after year, and are disease free.
Rodents leave them quite alone as well,
thank you.

The setting for the nostalgic garden opposite is a low, rocky promontory that juts
out into Blue Hill Bay, Maine. Its old-
fashioned charm suits the owner-designer,
who, as a child, used to sail past the point
and dreamed of one day building a house
and living there. Well, now she does. Near
the water's edge, the thin soil barely covers
the rocks, and lichens, mosses, and a scat-
tering of sedums carpet the ground. On
higher ground, an old crab apple tree
stands between the water and a flowerbed
planted with white phlox, hybrid Asiatic
lilies in a rainbow of colors, astilbe, salvia,
and *Lythrum salicaria* 'Morden's Pink', all
carefree perennials that adapt well to growing in soil pockets.

On Mrs. Thomas Hall's property in Northeast Harbor on Mt. Desert Island in Maine, the woods come right down to the water. A path that meanders down to the rocks below is landscaped with dwarf evergreen shrubs, which are perfectly suited to conditions along the Maine coast.

Surely Katie Dennis's garden overlooking Northeast Harbor is one of the area's most beautiful, with such old-fashioned favorites as hybrid Asiatic lilies, pastel-colored daylilies, *Liatris*, campanula, delphinium, and astilbe. Summers are rarely stifling in Maine, and so many plants that resent hot, dry climates, such as delphiniums, do very well here. Because of the late Maine spring, plants that are early bloomers farther south bloom in tandem with late spring and early summer perennials. The visual effect is stunning, as everything seems to be blooming at once. It is hard to resist a leisurely stroll down through Katie's garden to the water's edge.

Brian Beckman's house perches high above
the hustle and bustle of the fishing village
of West Point, Maine. On top of the rocky
ledge, where sturdy pines weather the off-
shore winds, he has planted a thriving vegetable garden in a mere one foot of added
top soil.

Seaside Landscapes

Close to the beaches on the barrier islands and in some areas of the coastal lowlands of the mid-Atlantic region, you will find yourself gardening in almost pure sand with a thin top layer of organic material. The Long Island garden below, designed by Dean Peterson and George Lynch, is very close in spirit to a natural landscape and contains nothing but natives, with the exception of Japanese black pine. American beach grass, beach plum, and bayberry are all found in the wild up and down the Atlantic coast. Needless to say, the maintenance required by a garden like this is minimal. All of the plants are both adapted to and useful for binding very sandy soil, and despite the lack of diversity of color and texture, the landscape is inviting.

On low-lying lands near the sea, you may encounter both freshwater bogs and salt marshes. Freshwater bogs can occur surprisingly close to oceans and bays. This mysterious, near primitive landscape at Fire Island Pines, designed by Ken Ruzicka, was a low-lying area subject to flooding during periods of heavy rain. Since the water table was a mere one foot beneath ground level, he removed the soil and created a pond. It is planted with edible wild watercress, *Nasturtium officinale*, which is native to the area (this is usually available at pet stores in the section devoted to tropical fish). Water loving Japanese irises and yellow flag irises, not in bloom at the time the photograph was taken, are also in evidence, along with many native plants.

At Carol Mercer's East Hampton garden, a large lawn leads down from the house to wetlands that edge a natural pond. Where the soil is damp, she has planted moisture-loving cultivars such as tall candelabra-form primroses (*Primula japonica* and *P. vialii*), Japanese irises, and ferns. The pond is lined with pale-pink wild roses, quite probably planted by birds. Where the ground is drier, astilbe, various grasses, and many other perennials that are averse to boggy conditions thrive.

I can't recommend installing a lawn in large open areas close to the sea where the soil is sandy, unless you also install a staff of gardeners to care for it. Some creative alternatives are suggested by this series of photographs, which juxtapose late spring and mid-fall views of Carol and Alex Rosenberg's garden in Water Mill, New York, designed by Washington-based landscape architects Wolfgang Oehme and Jim van Sweden working closely with the owners. In the first two views (above), a meadow of catnip rolls up to a planting of various pampas grasses that offer cool green throughout spring and summer, and begin to sport their flamboyant plumage at the end of August. Two other views show a meadow planted with a sea of *Sedum spectabile* 'Autumn Joy' in spring and mid-autumn. A Japanese yew (*Podocarpus macrophyllus* var. Maki) seems to mimic the changing color of the sedum.

The mid-Atlantic coast boasts many sunny days throughout the summer. Why not take advantage of the sun to grow flowers? In this garden in Water Mill, New York, belonging to David and Lucille Berrill Paulsen, designer Elizabeth Lear created a grand wildflower meadow. The oxeye daisies *(Chrysanthemum leucanthemum)* and corn poppies *(Papaver rhoeas)* are part of a seasonal progression of bloom that also includes blue bachelor's button, *Coreopsis lanceolata, C. tinctoria,* and black-eyed Susan.

In another Long Island meadow garden
blessed with abundant sun, designer Elizabeth Lear planted a grove of Bradford pears
to shade a charming gazebo. In the distance,
Coreopsis lanceolata and *C. tinctoria* bloom
amid fescue grasses and achillea.

Here, at a large Long Island seaside estate, Jane Lappin retained a group of native black cherry trees when she created the lawn that the client required. The graceful group echoes Matisse's masterpiece, *The Dance*. This is a good example of the way sea breezes lend character to tough trees by the phenomenon known as wind pruning.

The bluffs along Long Island Sound have a more moisture-retentive soil and are more conducive to shady woodland plantings than the terrain on the South Shore. The grassy path at the Donald Currie–Daniel Gladstone garden in Southold (above), on the North Fork of Long Island, is edged by many plants suitable for shady conditions. Several varieties of hosta, including the stunning blue giant *H. sieboldiana*, and blue-flowering periwinkle make a cool but unobtrusive background for the planting. The tall *Viburnum dilatatum*, with its dazzling clusters of red berries, which persist well into the winter, bears scented white blossoms in early summer.

The coast of northern New England is rocky and wooded, and fogs rolling in off the sea constantly water the ground. In a woodland area of Mrs. Thomas Hall's garden in Northeast Harbor, Maine, the characteristic outcroppings of ledge rock, rectilinear tree trunks, paths of shredded bark, and vast plantings of nurtured mosses evoke the tranquility of the moss garden at Saijo-ji in Kyoto, Japan. The tradition of Asian-style gardens on Mt. Desert Island goes back to the gardens designed by Beatrix Farrand for the Rockefellers in Seal Harbor in the 1920s.

Dorothy and Stephen Globus's garden, at Cornielle Estates on Fire Island, New York, on Great South Bay, is occasionally flooded with salt water during the winter. The combination of plants in this durable bed is quite harmonious, with silvery dusty miller, pale green *Sedum spectabile* 'Autumn Joy,' which is just beginning to show its pink summer color, variegated velvet grass, and Scotch broom. Trees include a corkscrew willow and a Russian olive. Brilliant orange marigolds, of a color difficult to use in most gardens, work quite well here, providing highlights for the scheme. Seaweed is gathered from the shoreline for mulch: not only is this practical, but it contributes to the very special seaside look of this pretty planting.

34

Designer Tish Rehill is known for her flamboyantly colorful plantings. This bed in a Southampton, New York, garden sets reds against yellows in a sea of green: purple-foliaged sand cherry, which she has contained by severe pruning, purple-leafed barberry, and startling scarlet *Crocosmia* 'Lucifer' for the reds; and black-eyed Susans and *Coreopsis verticillata* 'Zagreb' for the yellows. *Gaillardia × grandiflora* 'Bremer' is diplomatic. The white-flowered groundcover is *Mazus*.

Seaside Color

This beautiful garden, designed by Tish Rehill, shows the full effects one can achieve when working with the characteristic forms and colors of plants that are tolerant of the sandy soil of the mid-Atlantic seaboard. The plantings combine annuals in profusion (sunflower, cosmos, spider flower, dahlia, nicotiana, snapdragon), perennials (bugbane, astilbe, *Artemisia* × 'Powis Castle'), deciduous shrubs (*Spiraea* × *bumalda* 'Anthony Waterer'), and bulbs (hybrid Asiatic lilies). Notable are the use of grasses (including shimmering red-toned Japanese bloodgrass) where one would normally expect to find dwarf shrubs, and the absence of coniferous plants.

38

Baccharis (sea myrtle), with its silvery color and grey puffs of bloom, adds contrast to the rich early fall colors of Joanne Woodle's creek-front border.

Jane Lappin's beds for a Long Island summer estate hark back with good humor to English antecedents (both cottage garden and landscaped park), what with the amusing sheep grazing on the grass in the foreground. This is a planting that starts out tall and gets only taller, rising to spires of hollyhock that seem to look down even on the masses of sunflowers. A wide variety of familiar perennials includes bugbane, astilbe, daylilies, *Coreopsis grandiflora* 'Sunray,' *Phlox* 'Blue Boy,' and *Lythrum salicaria* 'Morden's Pink.'

The pool house at another Long Island summer estate landscaped by Tish Rehill is almost covered with very vigorous Japanese knotweed *(Polygonum cuspidatum)*, which is related to silverlace. In the adjoining border, she uses *Coreopsis* × 'Moonbeam,' old-fashioned *Petunia integrifolia*, and blue oat grass *(Helictotrichon sempervirens)* to produce a striking chromatic effect.

For this sweeping border leading up to the main house at a Southampton summer estate, Tish Rehill used hot colors—predominantly yellow, orange, and scarlet—for an effect that is almost jarring, particularly in the late afternoon, when this photograph was taken. She says that this palette is Mexican in inspiration, but it is remarkable how many yellow-flowered species thrive along the low-lying, sunny mid-Atlantic coast. Mrs. Thomas Hall's Maine woodland garden (pages 44–45), with not a yellow or orange flower in sight, makes an instructive comparison to this one. Among Rehill's favorite varieties are *Coreopsis* × 'Moonbeam,' *Pennisetum* 'Burgundy Giant,' Mexican sunflowers, and gaillardias (she favors G. × grandiflora 'Bremer,' 'Burgundy,' and 'Aurea Pura'). Notice how Rehill has achieved a layered effect using plants of different heights from the front of the border to the back.

Mrs. Thomas Hall's extraordinary garden looks out over Northeast Harbor, Maine. The perennial plantings are set among trees and shrubs, chiefly coniferous evergreens that thrive in the moist climate of coastal Maine, away from the dessicating winds and sandy soils of the mid-Atlantic seashore. Shrubs are sculpted into mounds and drifts in the Japanese manner, but the perennial borders are English in inspiration and the palette is limited to cool, largely pastel shades of pink, white, and blue. Among the favored varieties are astilbe (particularly *A. japonica* 'Rheinland'), annual white sweet alyssum, tall-growing meadowsweet (*Filipendula rubra* 'Venusta'), and Japanese and royal lilies. The blue end of the spectrum is held down by monkshood, an old-fashioned wild plant that has found its way into the most dignified and grand gardens the world over.

This lush planting of delphinium, astilbe, phlox, lilies, and liatris in a Maine garden (right) is a stone's throw from the water's edge. A pocket of earth has been turned into a dazzling perennial garden.

Green on green, two sago palms, wrought-iron urns, and a stone obelisk are an elegant and exotic touch in this Long Island garden.

An elegant antique wrought-iron bench painted white is in perfect scale for this small flower garden in Blue Hill, Maine, filled with such old-fashioned perennials as phlox, astilbe, campanula, daylilies, monarda, and, in the back of the border, a clump of bugbane, with its white, feathery flowers. Here, on the verge of a meadow, the slightly unkempt lawn with its crop of dandelions has a rustic charm. Farther away from the water is a cutting garden (below) planted with some of the same varieties.

The magnificent cutting garden at Carol Mercer's house in East Hampton, Long Island, provides for flower arrangements throughout the house beginning in early June and well into the fall. A weathered picket fence lends character to the pretty scene.

Pools and Ponds

Pools and ponds seem to invite plantings that are primarily cool in palette. Barbara Slifka's pool in Sagaponack, Long Island (left), is landscaped (by designers Wolfgang Oehme and Jim van Sweden) with clumps of ornamental grasses and plants with primarily blue-green foliage; perhaps it is the garden itself that chills "The Frigid Bather." Flowering plants are carefully chosen to echo the cool colors and simple forms of the grasses: along the edge of the pool, two ball-shaped blossoms of *Allium giganteum* nod over masses of deep-purple *Salvia* × *sylvestris* 'Mainacht.' Later in the season, globe thistle and catnip will carry on the cooling blue theme. In another Oehme–van Sweden garden (above), terra-cotta pots planted with cerise lantana, a tender perennial that can be moved indoors during the winter, are placed next to beds of Russian sage.

People will differ about the esthetics of building modern swimming pools by natural bodies of water. One design strategy is to make the pool as unobtrusive as possible. The plantings surrounding this swimming pool, by landscape architects Dean Peterson and George Lynch, establish a smooth transition from a tailored but informal garden built principally around dwarf conifers and massed perennials to the wetlands in the distance. Incidentally, the outer ring of pines is a good example of a windbreak.

Architect Dale Booher's and designer Lisa Stamm's own pool at their Shelter Island, New York, house is flanked by a curtained Turkish folly. If you look carefully inside the pool house, you'll notice that the interior is furnished with an upholstered banquette, far more comfortable to sit on after a swim than a wooden bench! Clumps of *Pennisetum* are installed here and there around the pool along with 'Betty Prior' roses, a single pink cluster-flowered variety that will grow virtually anywhere and flowers repeatedly through the summer—a good choice for seaside gardens.

58

People who choose to live or summer near the ocean often do so to be near water. Even the smallest property can have a lily pond, which can be anything from the focal point of a baronial garden to, well, a tiny garden in itself. The lily pond above, designed by Ken Ruzicka for a garden in Fire Island Pines, is planted with irises, calla lilies, and English ivy. The trellis that serves as a backdrop is rendered in cedar; it screens a graceful stand of bamboo.

Lily ponds can be quite small and still be marvelously effective. This gently gurgling pool on the terrace of Mr. and Mrs. Stockton Andrews's house in Bar Harbor, Maine, is planted with water lilies and a clump of Japanese irises, arranged with some black stones picked up along the coast.

Admirers often call this white garden in
Amagansett the Sissinghurst of Long
Island. A formal reflecting pool is the focal
point of a Romantic garden in the English
style; it is planted with water lilies and
banded bullrushes (*Schoenoplectus tabernae-
montani* 'Zebrinus') and surrounded by a
simple planting of irises and English ivy,
accented by two urns planted with a yellow
variegated variety of *Yucca filamentosa*.
When there were fish in the pool over the
winter, raccoons played havoc with it.

These two lily ponds on Long Island summer estates on the ocean show different approaches to landscape gardening when cost is not a consideration. Both gardens are within the sound of the sea, but from Tish Rehill's extravagant planting for the lusher of the two (left), one would hardly guess that the ocean is a short walk away. Particularly notable is Rehill's use of colorful annuals to complement the perennial plantings, among them tricolor sage (*Salvia viridis*), goldenleaf sage (*S. officinalis* 'Aurea'), globe amaranth (*Gomphrena globosa*), and various yellow-foliage plants. Jane Lappin's pastoral landscape for a lawn by the ocean (above) focuses more attention on the trees and the pool.

White wicker furniture on a porch with a view of the sea makes for a nostalgic, old-fashioned ambience. No less traditional is a foundation planting of hydrangea. Above, pompom-shaped French hydrangeas and pink Meilland roses are underplanted with dusty miller. The larger shrub on the left is a lacecap hydrangea (*H. macrophylla*). Designers Lisa Stamm and Dale Booher have captured another era with their garden for this Long Island house situated on a beach behind the primary dune.

In open, sunny locations, grasses can take the place of traditional shrubbery. The linear architecture of this Long Island guest house is echoed by several large clumps of maiden grass placed with geometric precision on either side of the deck. White Adirondack chairs and two pairs of planters of geraniums complete the scene. It looks as though the house has sprung up in the middle of nowhere, which is exactly where it is.

The patio at Donald Currie and Daniel Gladstone's house on the Sound Bluffs in Southold, New York, is dominated by a shadblow tree. The garden works its way with pleasing informality around and among the square flagstones. Here is a good example of diverse foliage forms and colors used together to good effect, including hosta, dwarf conifers, sedum, and grasses. Except for the yearly installation of tender annuals, the plantings require little maintenance.

White wooden tubs planted with Holly-wood juniper and pink hanging geraniums by designer Jane Lappin flank a doorway to a flagstone patio of a handsome house of white-rubbed brick. These junipers are very tough and can be left outdoors through the winter. As for privet, ivy, and hydrangeas, what is there to say? Gardeners on the East Coast have been combining them for over a century.

Here, as is often the case, the use of flagstones, along with wrought-iron furniture, gives the patio a more formal appearance. The ensemble, and the fountain in the brick wall that encloses it, are warmed by a perennial garden organized around four decorative urns with pink ivy-leafed geraniums spilling out of them.

67

The centerpiece of the elegant deck above, which was designed by Ken Ruzicka for a client in Fire Island Pines, is a beautifully pruned American holly planted in the ground beneath it. Other than the burgundy-leafed New Guinea impatiens in the large containers and the touch of geranium color on the roof of the guest house, the plantings are minimal, allowing the architecture, with its patterns of wood, to dominate the visual impact of the design. A purple-leafed flowering plum (*Prunus cerasifera* 'Thundercloud'), right, bears small pink blossoms in early spring and later little purple plums.

Growing through this deck by Ken Ruzicka is a thornless honey locust (*Gleditsia triacanthos* var. *inermis* 'Sunburst') with leaves that change from yellow in spring to bright green in summer. In July, highly fragrant white blossoms burst into bloom. The shade loving, pink-toned caladiums in the planter by the wall are an amusing match for the eccentric pink rocking chairs.

In many summer communities lot sizes frequently tend to be small and outdoor areas need to be screened for privacy. One common solution is the small deck with high walls, which can then be decorated with container plantings. These two examples, both by Ken Ruzicka for houses in Fire Island Pines, show formal arrangements and rely on those staples of seaside container planting: impatiens and geraniums. On one deck, below, the cascading Pronina junipers that look as if they are pouring out of their containers are quite extraordinary, as are the yellow-flowered marguerites (*Chrysanthemum frutescens*), which are trained as standards and, being tender, must be wintered indoors. The dwarf Alberta spruces together with the flamboyant mallows on the other deck, right, overturn one's expectation of the relative sizes of trees and flowers.

The word "deck" evokes a floor over water, which wouldn't be wrong in this case, since this structure, designed by Ken Ruzicka, overlooks a small freshwater pond. The pond was constructed of poured concrete, reinforced with chicken wire, and a colony of golden carp calls it home. The lush green planting of this tranquil spot includes cinnamon fern, English ivy, Piedmont azalea (*Rhododendron prinophyllum*), stonecrop (*Sedum spurium* 'Dragon's Blood'), creeping myrtle, candytuft, water lilies in the pond, and, for subtle touches of color here and there during the summer, white-blooming hosta and pale daylilies.

More easily than a garden, a deck or patio can be turned into an exotic stage set for a summer. The owner of the house above has enhanced the tropical ambience of a white canvas cabana hung with gossamer swags of white mosquito netting with pots of red hibiscus, yellow gazanias, and even a pineapple.

Contemporary architecture frequently calls for simple geometric plantings that seem to lack playfulness and joy. Here Jane Lappin uses a series of tubs planted with collections of different annuals to create a sense of orderly profusion. Each one is planted with flowers of two primary colors and the spectrum in between. For example, the blue-purple-red planter contains *Brachycome, Nemophila,* red dianthus, dwarf gaillardia, and blue *Nolana.* In another there are yellow, orange, and red lantana, verbena, and *Pentas lanceolata. Helichrysum* 'Limelight', a cascading foliage plant of chartreuse hue, is used to set off the annuals.

With a lattice ceiling for light, this protected area of Sandy and Larry Newman's seaside home in Amagansett, Long Island, is the perfect setting for these flower arrangements designed by MaryBeth Lee (left). Lee also created the stunning pot arrangement that accompanies the cement statue of the bloodhound (below). Wooly morning glory (*Argyreia nervosa*), a fast-growing annual vine that can grow up to 12 feet tall with leaves as much as 12 inches across, provides the backdrop to cascading geraniums, seashell impatiens, double impatiens, petunias, and sweet potato vine.

Don't think for a moment that patio plantings must be modest. Take this romantic niche for a traditional English garden bench on a flagstone terrace by a pool in Long Island. To say that the border behind the fieldstone wall, by designers Lisa Stamm and Dale Booher, is planted with mostly undemanding perennials seems to miss the point. It includes *Geranium sanguineum* var. *prostratum*, *Nierembergia repens*, *Coreopsis verticillata* 'Moonbeam', *Lythrum salicaria* 'Morden's Pink', allium, white astilbe, and 'New Dawn' climbing roses trained on structures inspired by *tuteurs* designed by Monet for his garden at Giverny. The classical-style garden urns are planted with heliotrope, which will bloom later in the summer, petunias, variegated geraniums, and *Helichrysum* 'Limelight.'

78

Paths, Fences, and Trellises

What boardwalks are to the mid-Atlantic coast, paths of pine needles and shredded bark are to the Maine coast. At the Thomas Hall garden in Northeast Harbor, one meanders up to an enchanting Japanese tea house that sits perched on the cliffs high above the water. This is truly a Maine forest look.

Boardwalks are a seashore institution. In Fire Island Pines, they are the only way to get around. The Pines retains many of the trees and shrubs native to the mid-Atlantic barrier islands, including pitch pine, sour gum, highbush blueberry, and the two species that characterize the mature barrier island forest as it can be seen in the nearby Sunken Forest National Seashore: American holly and sassafras. To compose the landscape seen here, Ken Ruzicka added white birch, P.J.M. rhododendron, *Rhododendron prunifolium*, andromeda, a single red maple, cinnamon ferns, hosta, *Bergenia*, water lilies, and daylilies. Groundcovers, including English ivy, *Lamiastrum galeobdolon* 'Variegatum,' snow-in-summer, and bugleweed, are used extensively. In the spring daffodils, clumps of lily of the valley, and Virginia bluebells (*Mertensia virginica*) add color to the scheme.

Round House, in East Hampton, Long Island, was designed and formerly owned by Jack Lenor Larson. The mature bamboo grove at the entrance to the house (opposite) towers over the path, creating a cooling effect during the hot summer days, as well as the deep shade favored by the many shade-loving perennials and groundcovers planted there today. The stark white stucco wall above, which separates the flower garden from the rest of the property, adds a cool touch in the deep shade. The laburnum tree, with its hanging yellow panicles, is traditionally paired with ornamental varieties of allium, which are sometimes difficult to grow. Chives, with their lavender blossoms, are an excellent and very practical substitute.

This elegant enclosed garden, designed by Lisa Stamm and Dale Booher, uses widely available annuals for color, in a palette that would have pleased Gertrude Jekyll herself: purple *Salvia farinacea* 'Victoria,' white nicotiana, and pink zinnias and cosmos. 'Heavenly Blue' morning glory climbs one of the tall trellises and box (*Buxus microphylla*) encloses the small parterres. Golden oregano (*Origanum vulgare* 'Aureum'), which is, of course, a culinary herb, edges the pathways.

The fence enclosing Mr. and Mrs. Stockton Andrews's Bar Harbor, Maine, garden, above, like the more refined fence, left, is a useful design for areas where deer are a problem, since it will discourage all but the most intrepid leapers but does not block out as much light as a solid fence. Many gardeners in summer communities add height to their fences by using bamboo poles instead of wood, which is heavier and more expensive. Here, the Japanese-style gate seems in keeping with the muted color tones of the planting, which includes pale lavender blooming hosta, white astilbe, and white Hybrid Asiatic lilies. Bolder colors are used only sparingly.

This enchanting gateway at Carol Mercer's East Hampton garden is covered with *Clematis* 'Will Goodwin' and wisteria. Wisteria has its advocates and detractors and comes in and out of style. One advantage of using it by the water is that salt spray and sand sap some of its legendary vigor, making it better behaved. The gate's lovely keyhole effect arouses one's curiosity. Who could resist opening it to see what is beyond in what feels like a very private place?

Designer Elizabeth Lear has used Nantucket ramblers ('Jeanne la Joie') with varieties of blue-flowering clematis over a moon gate in a Long Island garden. White double peonies bloom in front of a yew hedge.

English designer Charles Chesshire's clients in Amagansett longed for a "rose-covered cottage." He designed this planting on spanking white trellises. The roses that he selected include the climber 'New Dawn,' the hybrid musk rose 'Lavender Lassie,' which is actually rose-pink, and pink Meilland shrub roses. That's European dune grass under the stairs.

Another rose-covered cottage, this one in Water Mill, New York, was designed by Elizabeth Lear. To complement the pink 'New Dawn' climbing rose, she has planted *Viburnum plicatum* 'Watanabe,' hydrangea, pink dahlias, and white snapdragons.

Katherine and Ralph Tise, of Corneille
Estates, Fire Island, have decorated a shed
with trellises and planters and installed an
amusing bird house. Included in the planting are Montauk daisies, *Sedum spectabile*
'Autumn Joy,' dusty miller, purple loosestrife, and cosmos. The glossy leaved vine in
the upper left of the photograph is catbrier.

The little cottage above with its window boxes of pale pink and white annuals, on the grounds of an estate in Northeast Harbor, Maine, is a favorite hideaway of children when they come to visit. The charming birdhouse is always full during the season. For whatever reason, birdhouses are rarely used by landscape designers, but people who create their own gardens almost always make room for one. There are always a lot of birds looking for food and lodging along the Atlantic coastline.

Seaside Gardening:
A Practical Guide

For the purpose of this chapter, I assume that you've never really gardened before. In this spirit, I am providing you with some information to help you predict what will or won't grow in your garden, given the conditions in your area, and some basic procedures about how to plant and maintain a garden by or near the sea.

I have two primary pieces of advice. First, don't overreach. Gardening should be a satisfying and relaxing pursuit. Presumably, you are at the seashore to unwind, to spend time with your family and friends, to read, to swim, to do nothing, slowly. Second, remember that all good gardening practice involves a combination of experience and information. As soon as you begin to garden, you begin to acquire both (and often too much of the latter) from fellow gardeners, books, catalogues, magazines, and newspapers. For example, while clematis is a beautiful vine that's easy to grow; pruning instructions for clematis are about as easy to follow as an IRS form. Don't despair. Plant what you like and have reason to think will thrive, and observe the results. This is the pathway to wisdom.

ASSESSING THE SITE

As a gardener, you want to know what plants will survive and thrive in your garden. To answer this question, you must be familiar with the general climate, weather, soil, and water conditions of your area. In general, climate is a constant, while weather, soil, and water conditions may change dramatically along a coastline.

The Agricultural Research Service of the U.S. Department of Agriculture has divided the United States and Canada into eleven plant hardiness zones for the convenience of gardeners and farmers. These zones are determined by average annual minimum temperature. Overall climate is the one area in which seaside gardeners get a break over inland gardeners: because of the Gulf Stream, eastern coastal areas tend to be classified in higher zones than inland areas, and they experience the first killing frosts later in the fall as well. The Maine coast is considered to be in Zone 5 (–20° to –10° F), the Massachusetts coast to Cape Cod in Zone 6 (–10° to 0° F), and from Cape Cod south to the Chesapeake in Zone 7 (0° to 10° F). You will frequently see these zones mentioned in garden catalogues and books, and it's a good idea to plant varieties rated for your zone at first. That can change when you develop a thorough knowledge of your garden's microclimate: virtually every gardener knows someone who has a thriving specimen of a plant that allegedly can't be grown at that latitude. I have had great success in growing camellias, which usually have to winter under glass this far north, in my eastern Long Island garden. The oldest, a twelve-foot-tall *Camellia japonica*, is now in its twenty-seventh year.

Weather, soil, and water conditions along the Atlantic coast are much more difficult to predict. The sandy beaches and barrier islands that stretch from eastern Long Island south to the Carolinas offer very different opportunities to the gardener than Maine's rockbound coast, the Long Island bluffs overlooking Long Island Sound, or the coastline's numerous estuaries, tidewaters, and wetlands. One rule of thumb, though, is that the closer you are to the ocean, the more steps you will have to take to provide a protected environment for a garden.

There are, in fact, numerous discrete environments or habitats along the Atlantic coast, but the gardener can make do with a few general guidelines. I have adapted and simplified a classification from the Cornell Cooperative Extension Service of Suffolk County, New York. While it's important to choose plants able to endure the harsh environment, with careful design and horticulture, you can grow many more varieties of plants near the ocean than this advice suggests. Just look at many of the gardens illustrated in this book! Of the four "belts" listed here, the first three define areas directly on the water with differing soil conditions and exposure to wind and windborne salt spray. The fourth refers to coastal areas not directly on the water.

Ocean Beaches

Gardens directly on ocean beaches are very vulnerable to damage from wind, windblown sand, salt spray, and winter flooding, which few plants can tolerate year in and year out. Usually, unless they have been destroyed by development or storms, a system of dunes protects the land behind an ocean beach. Naturalists call the dune closest to the sea the primary dune. Plants that are native to the primary dune—in the northeast, mainly American beach grass—act as dune stabilizers, slowing the wind at the surface of the dunes and helping to gather windborne sand. During storms, their root systems help hold sand in place, slowing dune erosion. Any dunes behind the primary dune are called secondary dunes. The valley between the primary dune and the first secondary dune is called a swale. In practice, any property fronting an ocean beach is located in the swale (although in most cases, development has caused the leveling of secondary dunes to make way for more lots, and storms may have leveled the primary dune). The gardener directly on the ocean could do worse than work with what grows in the swale naturally—such as beach grasses, bearberry, bayberry, beach plum, groundsel, red cedar, rugosa roses, and seaside goldenrod—and adding different plants judiciously.

Barrier Islands, Salt Marshes, Bays, and Estuaries

Barrier islands, peculiar to the east coast of North America from Georgia to New York, are narrow, sandy islands that run parallel to the coast and are separated from it by shallow saltwater bays or lagoons. (Not all of the Atlantic islands are barrier islands. On bigger islands like Martha's Vineyard and Nantucket, for example, you will find a full range of seaside conditions.) On the barrier islands, there is far more exposure to breezes laden with salt spray than on the coastal plain, because the land itself is virtually at sea level. The "soil," such as it is, is almost entirely pure sand (in Fire Island's Sunken Forest National Seashore, the sand is overlaid with a layer of organic material—made up of humus and decayed plant material—that is all of six inches deep). Here, and this holds true as well for low-lying bayfront land on the mainland, there is an amazing range of conditions that can affect the gardener. Dry lands adjoining salt marshes or bays can be difficult to plant because salt enters the groundwater from the bay. Only a few feet farther inland, the groundwater will be fresh. In general, shallow-rooted plants will struggle to survive in sandy soil that does not retain water well.

Coastal Bluffs

Oceanfront properties atop sandy or rocky bluffs offer the gardener more options in terms of the variety of plants that will survive. The chief advantages conferred by elevation are that the soil will tend to be less sandy and there will be less exposure to salt spray during the growing season. For reasons having to do with the geological history of North America, you will find very little sand in the soil of Maine's coast.

Coastal Plains

The plain that stretches behind sand dunes or bluffs is naturally far more protected from wind, salt spray, and other natural forces, and usually offers less sandy soil as well. However, severe winter storms and hurricanes can carry salt water and gale-force winds many miles inland. The National Park Service estimates that in any one year, there is an 11 percent chance of a hurricane striking Long Island, and a northeaster will cause "significant damage" somewhere along its coast almost every year. As you move north, the chance of catching a hurricane diminishes, while the strength of winter northeasters increases.

If you have a garden on or near the sea, refer to the Plant Encyclopedic in the second half of this book to find plants that will grow where you live. I have compiled these lists with an eye toward including a diversity of species that, for one reason or another, are likely to thrive in the environments described above. In general, plants described as being drought resistant will probably adapt to the sandy soil of the barrier islands without special care and watering. Those that will grow reliably on ocean dunes or in bogs and wetlands are also noted. For further suggestions, consult with local nurseries and other gardeners.

Snow fences are deployed on primary dunes to help prevent dune erosion, above, while clumps of rugosa roses, left, take root in the swale. Along a low, sandy bluff on the north shore of Long Island, below, Montauk daisies, yarrow, and seaside goldenrod help to bind the soil.

One of the best ways to prevent erosion is to install soil-binding plants such as American beach grass (Ammophila breviligulata) or rugosa roses on waterfront property. Snow fencing can help as well, but sometimes nature will take its course

Wind and Erosion

Your first step in planning a garden by the water is to afford it the protection it needs from the elements. Windbreaks serve not only to protect plantings, but they also make the outdoor areas of your property more comfortable. But be careful not to make the mistake of blocking the view that drew you to the house in the first place. Sometimes it's helpful to take snapshots of the property and then sketch in the plantings that you envision, to see how they will frame the view. Keep in mind that the area in the lee of the house, that is, the facade that faces away from the water or the prevailing winds, is protected by the house itself and may be the best site for a garden.

When installing a natural windbreak, use the toughest plants for the outermost wind-exposed area. Then, as you progress in from the rim area, you can experiment with plants that are not as durable. Look under Shrubs and Trees in the Plant Encyclopedic for recommendations of what to plant for windbreaks. Remember that even the most rugged species of trees will have difficulty establishing themselves in highly exposed situations and once established will exhibit growth patterns that are markedly different than what you will find inland. Japanese black pine (*Pinus thunbergiana*), which is most often recommended for use as a shoreline windbreak (and which is now undergoing a blight along the East Coast), can grow up to 130 feet in optimal conditions, but would be hard put to attain 20 feet next to the ocean. In fact, a bulletin of the New York Cooperative Extension Service recommends protection by a shoreline windbreak even for this species.

If your property is directly on the water and thus subject to the extremes of winter weather and storms, it is a good idea to provide some protection for newly planted trees, shrubs, and hedges in mid-fall. In short, your windbreak has to become established or it will fall prey to the wind itself. To protect trees, first wrap the trunk with tree wrap. Then drive two stakes into the ground, one on either side of the trunk, leaning into the prevailing wind, and secure the tree to the stakes with old nylon stockings or rags (do not use rope, heavy-duty cord, or cable, as they will damage the trunk). Finally, and do this for newly planted shrubs as well, create a simple burlap cage to protect the branches. Drive wooden or metal stakes into the ground several feet from the trunk or main growth and then wrap burlap around the stakes to enclose the plant.

On oceanfront property, you must do what you can to build up the primary dune to protect your property from the erosion caused by storms and flooding, before thinking about windbreaks. In most coastal communities, the primary dune is subject to a complex web of laws and regulations. In New York State, for example, you cannot move sand from the beach to the dune without permits, which are difficult to get. New Jersey, as of this writing, places heavy restrictions on what can be planted within 150 feet of beaches, bays, and rivers between Sandy Hook and Cape May. Check your local town and state regulations.

If the dune is barren of vegetation, common snow fencing can be installed to trap windborne sand and help build it up, as described by R. Marilyn Schmidt in *Gardening on the Eastern Seashore*. Place one fence at the base of the dune parallel with the shoreline and perpendicular to the prevailing winds, and another no more than thirty feet above the first. Alternatively, you can run fencing perpendicular to the prevailing winds at thirty-foot intervals from a fence parallel to the shoreline. (More elaborate zigzag patterns are also employed in some communities.) In the spaces between the fencing, you should, at the very least, plant native American beach grass (*Ammophila breviligulata*), which spreads vigorously by underground roots. It is the fastest-growing of the beach grasses appropriate for our climate. Plant small clumps about eight inches deep from mid-fall to early spring. Set at eighteen-inch intervals in staggered fashion. Fertilize heavily with 10-10-10 fertilizer at the rate of 100 pounds per one-quarter acre in mid-spring and then again in mid-summer. Irrigate thoroughly to be sure that fertilizer gets to the roots of the plants. Some naturalists believe that a community of beach plants will hold the sand more effectively than beach grass alone, and that beach plum, groundsel, and seaside goldenrod, to name a few possibilities, should be planted with the beach grass.

Even if a garden is not directly on the water, some provision must be made to protect plants from wind. My garden is on the North Fork of Long Island, about one-quarter mile north of Peconic Bay and one-quarter mile south of Long Island Sound. The prevailing winds are from the west, and during the winter and well into the spring, they are nearly constant. I have screened the area with both a stockade fence and a dense hedge of Japanese holly, which provides substantial protection for my plantings, to the point that I have not found it necessary to mound my rosebushes, which are adjacent to the windbreak, during the winter. During the past thirty years or so, I have rarely lost a rosebush to the wind and cold of winter.

Salt Water

People living by oceans and bays whose gardens are frequently inundated with salt water, either from wind-blown salt spray or flooding associated with tides and storms, are naturally concerned about how the salt will affect their plantings. Curiously enough, inland regions of the American West, where soils in arid regions are naturally sandy and have high concentrations of salt, have provided the worst-case scenario. Horticulturist Fred D. Widmoyer reports, in the Brooklyn Botanic Garden's bulletin on soils, that high salt concentrations can cause "inhibited seed germination, stunted growth, leaf scorch, wilting, and death of the plant."

Fortunately, under normal weather conditions, the salt spray carried by the wind does not cause severe problems for most plants in seaside gardens. However, plants that are constantly exposed to large amounts of wind-borne salt spray will become less efficient at absorbing water from their roots and may sustain injury. For this reason, if an open spot on your seaside property regularly takes a beating from wind and waves, select and grow only the toughest and most salt-spray-resistant plants to grow there.

Plants that are native to seaside environments have adapted in various ways to salt spray. For example, you will notice that many recommended seaside plants offer silver or gray foliage. If you look closely at some of these plants, you will see that the silver color is created by a whitish fuzz, which protects the fleshy part of the leaf. Salt spray, which might otherwise damage the plant, is trapped in these minuscule hairs. Our native beach plums and bayberry sport fruit that is waxy to the touch. The waxy surface protects the berries, which are essentially seed containers, from the salt spray. Some other native plants, such as sea grape, sea holly, and yucca, have glossy, smooth foliage that repel water. Still others, such as willow, Russian olive, and sea buckthorn, have very small leaves that shed water more efficiently than large leaves. All of these adaptations, not incidentally, account for qualities that can give seaside gardens their distinctive appearance.

In *Gardening on the Eastern Seashore*, R. Marilyn Schmidt points out that some plants actually benefit from salt spray, which seems to control fungal and insect infestations in roses, hollies, Australian pine *(Pinus nigra)*, lilacs, and zinnias. Most plants are more susceptible to salt spray damage when the foliage is young—that is, in spring or early summer. Mercifully, most severe seaside storms, such as gales, hurricanes, and northeasters, occur during late summer and well into fall, when the foliage has matured and toughened. During such storms, salt water is swept up by the wind and released over the coast, sometimes many miles inland.

Beyond thinking ahead—by selecting plants that resist salt-spray damage—there are a number of ways to help plants recover from a heavy dousing of salt water. As soon as possible after a storm has passed, or even as it begins to wane, the most important thing to do is to hose down your plants, including trees, hedges, and tall shrubs, thoroughly and forcibly. Then flood the ground around them with freshwater. You want both to wash the plants and dilute the concentration of salt on the soil surface. Conifers and other evergreens usually sustain greater foliage damage than deciduous trees, since the plants do not drop their foliage in the fall.

If the salt spray dousing has been especially severe, deciduous trees may lose their foliage. This happened on the east end of Long Island and in Connecticut during September of 1987, when the severe winds of Hurricane Gloria came from the south, bearing much salt spray from the Atlantic Ocean, Long Island Sound, and Peconic Bay. Shortly after the storm passed, the leaves on the trees turned an ugly brown and fell to the ground. However, to everyone's amazement, the trees soon sported new buds, which then leafed out, creating a second spring. Many spring-blooming shrubs—forsythia, rhododendron, azalea, and lilac—also bloomed again that fall. The following spring, all was back to normal, and the plants displayed their usual glorious, colorful blossoms. After Hurricane Gloria struck, some of my neighbors did hose everything down to remove salt spray, but many who did not lost little, if anything, from their gardens. Waterfront properties suffered greater losses, although the long-term consequences of the storm, except where plants were uprooted or broken by the high winds, were not nearly as devastating as we had expected.

Severe storms often flood low-lying land at the seashore with saltwater. This rarely causes permanent damage to plants unless poor drainage causes it to stand on the soil. You can help by irrigating the plants as soon as the floodwater subsides with generous amounts of freshwater to wash the salt out of the soil, assuming that your drainage is good.

More serious is persistent saltwater flooding or the presence of salt in the groundwater. In planning seaside plantings, be aware of low-lying areas, try to ascertain whether or not they flood frequently, and plant salt-tolerant species if you are in doubt. The presence of the groundsel tree (*Baccharis halimifolia*), a native of coastal marshes that can tolerate high concentrations of salt around its roots, is often a sign that there is salt in the groundwater, usually from a nearby bay. Areas that flood regularly and retain standing water should be dealt with thoughtfully. Before you try to drain or fill in a bog or salt marsh, it is best to consult a professional landscape architect or engineer for advice. Remember, also, that laws may forbid filling in or altering the wetland and estuary areas of the seaside environment.

Soil and Sand

Sand is not soil. Of the sixteen elements known to be essential to the growth of most plants, thirteen—that is, all but carbon, hydrogen, and oxygen (and some of the nitrogen)—originate in the parent rock from which soil develops. The white sand beaches characteristic of the Atlantic coast south of Maine are 98 percent weathered particles of quartz, a medium that is unusually poor in the minerals that most plants need. The closer you are to the seashore, the more sandy—and poorer in elements essential for plant growth—your soil is likely to be.

Furthermore, without constant watering during the summer, plants that are not drought resistant tend to dry out quickly in sandy soil, suffering severe stress. Prevailing winds cause them to lose moisture rapidly through their leaves, and they are growing in a medium that does not retain moisture effectively around their roots. To improve the moisture retentiveness of sandy soil and to provide necessary nutrients, it must be enriched with organic matter: humus, compost, peat moss, decayed leaves, or topsoil. Many seaside gardeners grow rapturous about the value of seaweed—the eelgrass (*Zostera marina)* that washes up in vast quantities on bay shores along the Atlantic coast and is free for the taking—as a mulch and soil builder. It is indeed an excellent mulch, and does not need to be washed with freshwater as many gardeners seem to believe. But its one drawback as a soil builder is that it contains very little nitrogen and decomposes slowly. If you want to try to improve your soil with seaweed alone, also add an extra source of nitrogen, like fish meal. The more organic matter you add to sandy soil, the greater the variety of plants you will be able to grow. As a rule, you should excavate areas you plan to plant to a depth of one foot and mix the excavated soil with about one-half to two-thirds as much organic material (see Planting and Maintaining Hardy Plants, page 103).

Most gardeners learn about their soil and what can and can't grow in it by experience and observation. For example, you might be concerned about the pH value of your soil since you will occasionally see it mentioned that a certain plant is known to prefer acidic soil or alkaline soil when you browse through catalogues or books. The relative acidity of a soil can be ascertained by testing, but it's not something you should worry about unless you have reason to think that there is a problem with your soil. (In general, soils in the eastern United States tend to be acidic, but sandy seashore soil is often alkaline.) If you're worried about soil problems, you can have your soil tested by your local County Extension Service, which you can find by looking in the telephone directory under County Offices. There is usually no charge for this service, and the experts will not only test the soil but provide recommendations about how to go about improving it and suggestions of what to grow.

If your soil is very sandy, and you can't afford to improve it on a large scale, you can create pockets of improved soil throughout your property. Another alternative is to build raised beds on top of the soil, making containers for good soil using treated lumber, bricks, stone, or even concrete. If you need to clear a space for a garden and you want to embark on a long-term soil improvement program, consider recycling the brush, twigs, and leaves that accumulate on your property rather than having them carted away. You can hire a local garden service to clear, chip, and shred this material, and you will be surprised to see how it breaks down into soil over time. Finally, do not overreach: remember, beautiful and distinctive gardens have been created using only varieties that are completely adapted to seaside conditions, planted in sandy soil enriched with seaweed.

Special Care for a Seaside Garden

If you want to grow any plants other than native species in the sandy soil of the Atlantic coastline south of Maine, there are certain steps you should take to ensure that they are protected against loss of precious moisture and receive the nutrients that they need.

Beyond adding organic matter to sandy soil to improve moisture and nutrient retention, there is another way to conserve moisture: use mulch! The soil around all plants should be covered with at least two to three inches of organic mulch. Not only will this protective layer serve to conserve moisture and reduce the concentration of surface salt by slowing water evaporation from the soil, but it will also cut down on weed growth and, as the organic material breaks down, it will add nutrients to the soil.

There are many different materials that you can use for mulch, and your choice will depend in part on what is available and what you think looks good. The best is homemade compost (which is simply

The view toward the wetlands adjoining Carol and Alex Rosenberg's house in Water Mill, New York, above, is a meadow of reeds, Phragmites australis, *a Middle Eastern native that may be the most broadly naturalized plant in the world. While it would be unwise to plant reeds (many naturalists lament that they are everywhere crowding out native species), it is often the better part of wisdom to leave them undisturbed in wetland areas unless you are really adept at gardening with natives.*

decomposed plant residues, usually mixed with manure). With a little bit of effort and planning, you can have large supplies of what gardeners call "brown gold" at a very good price . . . for nothing. Even if you don't purchase or build a composter, you can simply make a compost pile in an inconspicuous corner of your garden by alternating six-inch layers of organic plant material, including wet vegetable garbage from the kitchen such as coffee grounds and vegetable parings, along with leaves, grass clippings, seaweed, and weeds, mixed with some soil, and two-inch layers of manure. The pile should be roughly flat or concave on top, to conserve as much moisture as possible. Experience shows that you need about a cubic yard of material to generate compost. After a season or so, you will have plenty of compost to enrich the soil and to use as mulch.

Oak leaves and pine needles provide an airy cover for the ground and improve the soil. Other leaves, such as maple leaves, tend to mat on the surface of the soil and can be harmful to plants unless they are reduced to compost. A two-inch layer of beach stones can be quite attractive around trees, hedges, or shrubs that are growing within the brickwork of a patio. They will help to conserve moisture and keep the weeds down, although they do not add nutrients to the soil. Eelgrass also makes an excellent mulch.

If you opt to purchase mulch from a nursery, garden center, or landscaping service, it's probably best to choose salt hay or wood chips, usually cedar or pine, in the smallest size you can find. Although the large chips may look reasonably attractive, they do not decompose readily enough. If you use wood chips, you should be aware that they will monopolize the nitrogen available to your plants while they decompose, so fertilize accordingly. Buckwheat hulls are too light to use in windy seaside environments, as are cocoa shells, which can be somewhat distracting in a garden on account of their chocolate scent. I cannot recommend grass clippings or peat moss.

Fall plantings should be protected by a six-inch layer of mulch to protect them over the winter. While hardy plants will not be harmed by the cold, constant freezing and thawing of the surrounding soil can cause them to heave up out of the ground. Salt hay keeps the soil at a more constant temperature, making it less likely that a plant will heave.

Well-mulched soil retains moisture well, but during prolonged periods of summer drought, you will still need to water to a depth of a foot to a foot-and-a-half at least once a week. Check this by digging a place in the garden where plants do not grow, but which has been watered. Lay down drip hoses, available at garden and home improvement centers, in your garden and leave them there for the growing season. These are preferable to conventional sprinklers, which lose water to evaporation and run-off. If local ordinances prohibit watering, you need to be especially careful to plan your garden using only the most drought-tolerant species.

Finally, you should fertilize your plantings, particularly if you are gardening with non-native species. For best results, work about one tablespoon per square foot of all-purpose 5-10-5 fertilizer into the soil around each plant each spring before growth commences. If your soil is decidedly sandy, you should fertilize more frequently, because inorganic nutrients leach out of sandy soil very rapidly. Be careful not to overfertilize. More often than not, fertilizer runs off into the groundwater, where it can do more harm than good.

Planting and Maintaining Hardy Plants

Although spring is usually when gardeners install new plantings of shrubs, hedges, trees, and perennial plants, early fall is also a good time. A plant's roots continue to grow until the very cold days of January or February—long after the rest has gone dormant—and a strong root system is what a plant needs to endure the dry heat of summer. Seashore areas, where seasonal temperatures are sustained almost a

An aerial view of the Hereford Inlet Lighthouse and Gardens at Wildwood, New Jersey. To help the garden survive the harsh Atlantic winds, designer Steve Murray has surrounded the property with salt-tolerant Japanese black pines.

month longer than inland, offer sites for fall planting, with the exception of very exposed locations, which should be planted in the spring so that the plants have the summer to acclimatize. You should probably forgo the pleasure of fall planting on low-lying land by the water and on barrier islands as well. By the way, it is especially necessary to mulch fall plantings to guard against winter heaving.

Planting the tree, shrub, or other plant is easy. Just remember that the hole should be twice as wide as the root ball. It should be deep enough for the bottom to fit snugly and the top to be slightly above ground to allow for settling. Start by removing the soil, and then position the plant in the hole and fill in beneath and around the roots (or root ball), tamping the soil and watering as you work, to ensure that you don't leave any air spaces. When you are done, water the plant thoroughly and tamp the soil firmly. Water once more. Be sure to leave a slight depression in the soil around the plant to facilitate watering throughout the season.

Give your plants growing space. Don't cramp shrubs and trees. In perennial plantings, a good rule of thumb is that tall-growing plants should be planted two feet apart, medium-height plants eighteen inches apart, low-growing plants twelve inches apart, with tiny, miniature plants perhaps six inches apart.

Most plants need very little care beyond watering and feeding. The one chore you should make a habit of is to deadhead your perennials, that is, remove the spent blossoms. Not only does this make the plants look better, but in some cultivars, it helps to produce a second bloom. You don't deadhead flowering trees and shrubs (thank goodness), but you should remove old flower heads from lilacs, azaleas, and rhododendrons to improve next season's blooms. Unruly shrubs and vines can be pruned in the spring, with the exception of certain plants that bloom only from old wood and should be pruned right after flowering—experience and the specific horticultural instructions that come with each plant are good teachers in this regard. Always prune damaged trunks and branches in the aftermath of a storm.

Remember, no plant is immortal. When a perennial becomes overgrown or seems to have lost its vigor, dig it up in the spring, divide it (that is, break the crown gently into several pieces, each with its own roots), and replant what you want to keep. Give the rest to an aspiring gardener down the street.

Containers

You can grow virtually anything in containers, including plants that won't normally thrive in typical seaside conditions, as long as they are watered regularly. Many tropical and subtropical plants, which are not hardy in northern climates, can be grown outdoors in containers in the summer and then brought indoors to a greenhouse or a sunny area in the house for winter enjoyment. Just remember that a small pot in full sun in hot weather may need watering once a day. If you can't be around to water that often, try filling a large container with peat moss, wet it thoroughly, and place a smaller container planted with annuals in the middle. You can mask the edge of the smaller container with more peat moss.

The range of containers available is vast, and imaginative gardeners use just about anything that will hold soil to grow plants. The only essential thing is to be sure to provide drainage holes and a one-inch layer of pebbles or flowerpot shards in the bottom of the container for drainage. Beyond that, a simple soil mixture that is highly retentive of moisture is called for, either one-third garden loam, one-third compost, and one-third peat moss or one part garden loam to one part vermiculite or perlite. Before planting, thoroughly soak the planting medium. Most gardeners plant their containers in the spring after all danger of frost is past. While they are occasionally used for herbs, scented geraniums, and perennials, containers are usually planted with annuals. See the section on Tropicals & Tender Perennials in the Plant Encyclopedic for more on gardening with containers.

Pests

Many insects, reptiles, birds, and animals are the gardener's friends. Ladybugs, wasps, praying mantises, and fireflies consume not only the eggs of many harmful insects, but in some cases kill the insects themselves. Birds offer colorful plumage and lovely songs, and some eat their weight in insects every week. Bats also are great insect eaters, consuming thousands of mosquitoes a day. Bees pollinate flowers and make honey. Butterflies add much beauty to the garden. Toads consume ticks and many other harmful insects;

Remedies for Common Insect and Fungal Infestations

Aphids are small green insects that suck juices from buds, then leaves, then stems. Malathion is effective in the short term while Sevin useful for longer protection.

Lace bugs are small bugs with large, lacy wings that attack azaleas, hawthorn, and other plants. Leaves appear mottled. Spray regularly with Malathion, according to manufacturer's directions. If you wish to use a natural repellent, spray with rotenone or pyrethrum according to manufacturer's directions.

Leafhoppers are wedge-shaped insects that attack many plants. Leaves may turn pale or brown and growth will be stunted. Malathion is the chemical spray to use, pyrethrum the botanical spray.

Mealybugs are white cottony insects that attack many plants. Growth is stunted. Sevin is the chemical spray to use and, although it is not as effective, spraying daily with a half-and-half solution of water and detergent for about a week may help.

Mildew is mold that forms on the foliage of some plants, particularly zinnias, monarda, deciduous azaleas, and phlox. To combat it, spray regularly from midsummer to fall with Captan or Benomyl, following manufacturer's instructions.

Mites are minute sucking insects that attack almost all plants. Leaves will be discolored. Use Sevin, or try spraying daily with a half-and-half solution of water and detergent for about week.

Red spider mites do not usually appear until the heat of summer. Plants become yellow and weak and the undersides of leaves look dirty because soil sticks to the fine webs that the mites weave. The webs first appear near the ribs or margins of leaves and then over entire surface, and the larger mites can be seen with the naked eye. Spray with Malathion.

Scale are tiny, usually hard, oval insects that attack many plants. Leaves will yellow and drop. Short of using the highly toxic Diazinon, spray with a half-and-half solution of water and detergent, which may help.

Snails and slugs attack many plants and eat the foliage. Set a shallow aluminum pie plate filled with beer near the plants being attacked. Slugs love beer: they will climb into the pie plate and drown.

Thrips are tiny, winged insects. Leaves become silvery. The chemical cure is Malathion; the botanical spray is rotenone.

snakes eat rodents, such as moles and voles. If you have an outdoor pet cat, he too will help to keep moles and voles under control.

However, not everything in nature loves a garden. If your plants do not look healthy, inspect them carefully to determine what may be the problem. Use a magnifying glass to expedite diagnosis. The list on page 105 gives remedies for the most common insect and fungal infestations. If you opt for chemical treatments, which are available at most nurseries and garden centers, always follow the manufacturer's instructions, to protect your health and the environment. In many seaside communities, the water table is high and chemicals are rapidly passed to it through the upper soil layer, so you should take special care when using pesticides and fungicides.

If you decide you do not want to use synthetic chemical sprays, use botanical sprays, which are made from plant materials. (Keep in mind that they are still toxic and do not discriminate between "good" and "bad" insects.) Rotenone and pyrethrum are both effective.

Beyond that, many insects can be controlled with a spray made up of a half-and-half solution of dishwashing detergent and water. However, don't expect a single application to rid your plants of pests. You will have to persist and spray every day for a week or so, and even then results are not guaranteed.

Small Animals

Rabbits and other small mammals are particularly hungry during the early days of spring, when plants that make up their normal diet may not have leafed out yet. They eat what they can, just to survive. Now we all have some compassion for their hunger, but not when they level the emerging buds of our autumn dreams, the bulb plantings that we worked so hard at planting last fall. Be thankful for small favors: they don't like daffodils, narcissus, crown imperial, snowdrops, *Iris reticulata, I. danfordiae,* lily of the valley, and scilla. They are ravenously addicted to crocuses and tulips. How many times have gardening friends told you that rabbits absolutely leveled every one of their emerging crocuses and/or tulips to the ground? I know gardeners who have totally given up on planting tulips and crocuses for this very reason.

However, take heart, for there are humane solutions. Dried blood, available in garden centers by the bag, works for me. Beyond repelling our friends with the big ears, it is excellent fertilizer for bulb plantings. As soon as you see the tiny green shoots of crocuses or tulips emerging from the ground—as early as late January—sprinkle some dried blood on the planting. Then, after each rain, and you must be meticulous about this, repeat the application. I've done this for the past twenty years or so and now have established plantings of crocus and even tulips that have perennialized. I have also found that laying small pieces of chicken wire over a planting until the buds open works. Rabbits just don't seem to want to walk on wire mesh, and I can't say that I blame them. I remove the mesh when the crocuses bloom and when the tulips reach about eight inches in height, carefully slipping it over the blossoms. If you notice that new growth on some of your perennials is being eaten, try the dried blood and chicken wire treatment until the foliage and emerging buds are about a foot high.

Unfortunately, dealing with moles and voles is not as easy. If you find yourself walking on grass that seems to sink beneath your feet or if there are long ridges of crumbled soil on the lawn, you probably have an infestation of moles. Moles tunnel beneath the ground in search of insect grubs, which usually congregate around the roots of grass, plants, or bulbs. The moles eat the grubs, but leave the plants alone. The only way you can get rid of the moles is to get rid of the grubs, which involves spreading all kinds of poisonous insecticides on the soil surface.

"Well, if the moles don't eat the bulbs, why should I worry?" you ask. Sometimes nature plays funny tricks. At work here is an insidious conspiracy, for after moles make holes in quest of the grubs, voles (which resemble mice) use the holes and tunnel through to the roots of plants and bulbs. Like the rabbits, they leave certain bulbs quite alone, thank you very much, but most are three-star fare as far as they are concerned.

Before I learned how to frustrate them, I had installed about one thousand bulbs, major and minor, in a rock garden. The sandy soil, nicely warmed by the rocks, was child's play to the moles and voles. All of the bulbs bloomed the first spring, and then through the summer and fall the voles cleaned out the entire planting. The next spring all that came up were the snowdrops, daffodils, and scilla. A friend of mine, who had installed an extravagant bed of tulips, was strolling through his garden with friends one days, admiring the planting. Suddenly, right before their eyes, one of the tulips disappeared into a hole in the ground.

I had read somewhere that if you lined planting holes for tulips, crocus, and other favored bulbs with mesh gutter wire, it would frustrate these creatures. I tried it and it did help somewhat, but by the second year, most of my bulb plantings still were cleaned out. Then, several years ago, I was in northern Portugal at the garden of vintner Antonio Guedes and I noticed the mole-made ridges in his lawn. I asked Guedes if he had mole and vole problems and he told me that he did, but that he had come up with a solution. Wherever he wanted a planting of tulips, he excavated the area, then sunk heavy-duty plastic or rubber pots into the soil, with the rim of the top at soil level. These pots all have drainage holes, necessary for any plant container, as professional growers use them to ship and sell perennials, shrubs, and trees. He would fill them with soil and plant as usual. I tried it in my rock garden and it worked. I have several plantings of species tulips which are now in their fifth year, apparently vole proof.

Voles not only attack spring-blooming bulbs, but fruit trees, some perennials, shrubs, and ornamental trees. There isn't really much you can do about them: if a healthy plant suddenly seems to expire, chances are the voles are eating the roots.

In some seaside environments, notably those along the rocky coast of Maine, or the Connecticut and Long Island shores of Long Island Sound, chipmunks chew away at many varieties of plants. Like moles and voles and rabbits, they savor crocuses and tulips. They also eat many varieties of annuals and perennials. Mrs. Thomas Hall, of Northeast Harbor, Maine, has come up with a kind solution to preserve the plantings in her stunning Japanese garden. She catches the chipmunks in Havahart traps, drives them several miles from her house, and releases them. Although she still has some chipmunk damage, trapping and transporting help somewhat.

Deer

Now we are talking big game. On Fire Island, off the coast of Long Island, deer are ubiquitous and wander through the various resort communities unafraid of human beings. They are very tame, will approach you for a handout, and have learned how to open garden gates that are not securely latched. Once inside a garden, they eat almost everything in sight. In other areas of seaside Long Island, where they are not quite so contained, they have also become quite blasé about human beings, sitting around and sunning themselves like odalisques on waterfront decks. The story is the same up and down the East Coast: deer populations have risen dramatically in residential areas over the past twenty years.

Although studies have attempted to determine just what plants deer like or dislike, none are conclusive and all are riddled with practical contradictions. Deer do prefer some food over others, but when their preferred food is in short supply and they are in danger of starvation, deer, like any living creature, will eat just about anything that grows in order to survive (as the Dutch ate tulip bulbs during the German occupation of Holland).

Beyond installing tall fences (see pages 84–85)—they must be at least seven feet high to keep deer out—or electric fences, there are some steps you can take to protect your plants. All newly installed trees and shrubs should be wrapped with tree wrap or Tubex, available at garden centers and nurseries and from many mail-order companies. Deer are particularly hungry at the end of winter and in early spring, when there are few foliage plants around to sustain them. Provide some sort of cage fencing for any favorite plants that you wish to protect.

Deer repellents like Ropel, Chew-Not, Deer Away, Bobex, Hinder, Plantskydd, and Liquid Fence are available at garden centers and nurseries. They may work if you follow the package directions very carefully and start application before the damage is done. You need to reapply often, particularly after rain or snow may have washed the deterrent from the plants.

More to the point, it makes sense to select plants that deer do not usually like to eat, although even this often does not work, for deer will develop a taste for a particular plant if they have had to eat it during famine periods.

Unfortunately, the intense debate about the widespread presence of deer in residential areas up and down the East Coast is finally not about nibbled plantings. To understand why so many gardeners are troubled by the presence of white-tailed deer, one need only turn to the publications of the Suffolk County, Long Island, Department of Health Services on Lyme disease, which are all decorated with bold drawings of stags.

Ticks and Lyme Disease

You must protect yourself against Lyme disease (first identified in Old Lyme, Connecticut, in 1975) and learn to recognize the symptoms if you garden along the East Coast. The disease is caused by a bacterium and is transmitted primarily by the deer tick. The ticks rest on vegetation and cling to humans or animals (mostly deer or field mice) as they pass by. The disease has been reported in almost every state, but it is most prevalent in eastern coastal areas from Maine to New York.

Lyme disease is sometimes difficult to diagnose. Deer ticks are very small—the nymph is about the size of a poppy seed—and people rarely notice them on their bodies until after they have been bitten. The most characteristic early sign of Lyme disease is the appearance of a rash at the site of the tick bite that slowly expands during the ensuing weeks. It may become as large as fifteen inches in diameter, but it will vary from person to person and not all people who get Lyme disease will develop the rash. Even if untreated, the rash will eventually fade. Other early symptoms of the disease are fever, headache, neck stiffness, muscle and joint pains, enlarged lymph glands, conjunctivitis, or even general fatigue.

On Fire Island, New York, gardeners face not only the challenges of poor soil, strong winds, and salt spray but also the ever-present deer.

The Charles Simon garden in Seaview on Fire
Island was especially designed with the collab-
oration of the late Jimmy Viles to welcome deer,
and the owner puts out trays of food to attract
the beautiful animals. It is essentially a bamboo grove with the addition of some conifers.

It is unwise to leave the disease untreated. The most common late complication of untreated Lyme disease—coming weeks to months after the initial infection—is swelling and pain in the large joints, especially the knees. In 15 to 25 percent of untreated patients, neurological complications may eventually occur, and fewer than 7 percent of untreated patients develop irregular heartbeats or other cardiac problems.

If you are bitten by a tick or if you think you might have Lyme disease, you should consult a doctor right away. Prompt treatment with antibiotics is usually effective.

There is no way for active gardeners to completely protect themselves against tick bites in areas with deer and rodent populations. The spring, when the ticks are smallest and most difficult to detect, is precisely when most gardeners are busiest and least in the mood to take cumbersome precautions. However, certain measures should become habitual: wear light-colored clothing with long pants and sleeves tucked into socks and gloves when you garden in areas with underbrush; check yourself and your companions or children once a day for ticks; check your pets regularly for ticks; consider using tick repellents containing the chemical DEET on your clothing (following the instructions carefully).

You can also try to manage your property so that the potential deer tick population is reduced. Deer ticks are found in heavily shaded, damp areas with abundant leaf litter and undergrowth, where their host animals also congregate. Fence deer out; mulch borders and shrubbery carefully; remove leaf litter from areas where you will be gardening or relaxing; and admire the brush-covered areas of your property from afar and try to keep kids and pets out of them.

Certain pesticides can be used to curb the tick population, but most of us are uncomfortable with the idea of exposing ourselves, our loved ones, and our neighbors to their possible long-term effects. One habitat-targeted product is Damminix, which is disseminated in cotton balls that mice use as nesting material; it is the equivalent of dusting field mice with tick powder. You also may want to consider spraying your clothing with the active ingredient in Damminix, permethrin, which kills ticks on contact. Please remember to follow the instructions carefully.

Deer and Plantings

The Cornell Cooperative Extension and the New York Cooperative Fish and Wildlife Research Unit have found that the following plants are rarely or seldom bothered by deer. People who live in areas with large deer populations and comparatively little native foliage—that is, on the shore—may find that the results of this study are overly optimistic. Here are some of their findings:

Annuals: ageratum, cleome, dahlia, dusty miller, forget-me-not, heliotrope, marigold, morning glory, parsley, poppy, snapdragon, sweet alyssum, sweet basil, verbena, wax begonia.

Perennials and bulbs: amsonia, astilbe, baby's breath, balloon flower, bergenia, bleeding heart, candytuft, cinnamon fern, columbine, coreopsis, crown imperial, daffodil, evening primrose, feverfew, goldenrod, heath, heather, lamb's ear, lavender, lily of the valley, oregano, oriental poppy, ostrich fern, painted daisy, partridgeberry, plumbago, purple coneflower, ribbon grass, rosemary, royal fern, sage, Shasta daisy, tiger lily, yarrow, yucca.

Groundcovers: ajuga, aurinia, lamium, pachysandra, vinca.

Vines: bittersweet, clematis, honeysuckle, wisteria.

Plant Encyclopedic

The following list includes plants that can be recommended for seashore planting on the East Coast of North America. Species that are especially suited to the seashore environment, particularly those with a high tolerance of drought, bear the symbol ❧. Within that group, plants that can survive directly on dunes are also noted. In general, plants described as being drought resistant will probably adapt to the sandy soil of the barrier islands without special care and watering.

Experienced gardeners will, no doubt, be able to point to many plants that are missing from this list, and it is not intended to be exhaustive or exclusive. Rhododendrons and azaleas, for example, are among the easiest of flowering shrubs to grow if you have a bit of light shade and a moisture-retentive soil; they are shallow rooted, however, and do not generally do well in dry, sandy soil, bright sun, and dessicating winds, and so they have been omitted. This should not be taken to mean that you cannot, with a bit of care, grow a rhododendron near the sea.

A word about native plants: the word "native" in this list is used generally to describe plants that are native to the East Coast. It is useful to know which plants are naturally adapted to the conditions in which you are gardening.

Annuals

I am a great believer in using annuals in the garden. Annuals are plants that live for one season, completing their life cycle—from seed to flower to seed—in this short span of time. Almost all annuals bloom throughout the summer and early fall, and some continue past the first frost.

Annuals are indispensable to the seaside gardener, who must see every year as a fresh start. How many gardeners have returned in the spring to their houses on the shore to find that winter storms and flooding have buried their perennial beds under drifts of sand and stunted vines that were once engines of growth? What a pleasure to contemplate the possibility of planters full of impatiens or a wall covered with morning glories. Even the summer renter can create a private paradise of annuals.

There are two ways to have annuals for your seaside garden. The first is to purchase seeds and grow the plants yourself, but it's hardly necessary. Instead, take advantage of the constantly expanding selection of seedlings and plants available at garden centers and nurseries. Selections used to be quite limited, but things have changed.

Taking care of annuals is a breeze. Most prefer full sun and are not fussy about soil. Plant and mulch as you would perennials, keeping in mind that annuals that are quite small at planting time can grow very quickly.

Designer Marla Gagnum created this charming cottage-style cutting garden for her clients David and Jeannie Orenstein in East Hampton, New York. After the roses and perennials have peaked, annuals continue the spectacular displays of color. The plants include cosmos, dahlia, ageratum, and zinnia.

A colorful planting of annuals and beach plums sits just a few yards from the ocean on the seawall.

Annual plantings are, to a great extent, maintenance free. Just remember to deadhead spent blooms, that is, cut faded flowers before they go to seed both for the sake of appearance and also to extend their period of bloom. Once seeds have formed, the plant has accomplished its purpose—to regenerate—and it will stop flowering. By deadheading, you frustrate this process and keep the plant blooming until frost.

All of the following annuals can be grown in all climates until a light or killing frost, depending on variety.

Ageratum houstonianum (floss flower)

Clusters of soft, powder-puff blossoms in various blue shades, as well as white and pink. Medium-green foliage. 6–24" depending on variety. Thrives in partial shade or full sun, in ordinary soil. Needs some moisture. Deadhead throughout season for continuous bloom. *Ageratum* combines well with pale-yellow–blooming and silver-foliaged plants. Recommended cultivars: 'Compact Blue' (true blue, 8–12"), 'Redtop,' 'Neptune Blue,' and 'Summer Stars.'

Antirrhinum (snapdragon)

Spikes of single, double, and butterfly-shaped blossoms in all colors except true blue. Medium-green foliage. 6–48", depending on variety. Thrives in full sun, in enriched alkaline soil, but will tolerate some shade. Start indoors under lights eight weeks before the last frost date in your area. Surface sow. Do not cover seeds, as light is needed for germination. Plant seedlings outdoors after all danger of frost. Pinch tips of plants when about 3" tall to encourage branching. Then pinch again when new shoots are 3" tall. For continuous bloom, deadhead spent flower stalks. Snapdragons often winter over in moderate climates. Cut back at the end of the flowering season and the plant will rebloom; usually the second year's bloom is even more spectacular than the first. Because taller varieties must be staked, select from dwarf or medium-height varieties. Available in wind-tolerant semi-dwarf varieties that are perfect for seaside, windy conditions, in red, white, rose, red/white, lavender, light pink, bronze, pink, yellow, and purple. Recommended for the worst seashore conditions.

❧ *Arctotis* (African daisy)
Brilliant yellow, salmon, apricot, orange, or white daisylike flowers. Gray woolly foliage. 12". Usually sold as color mixtures. Thrives in full sun and well-drained soil. Drought resistant. Seedlings resist early spring cold. Sow seeds in situ as early in spring as ground is workable. Cover seeds with soil or planting medium according to package directions. For continuous bloom, deadhead spent flower stalks.

Begonia semperflorens-cultorum hybrids (wax begonia)
Pink, salmon, coral, red, white, or bicolor clusters of blossoms. Stiff, waxy deep-green or bronze-toned, rounded foliage. 3–12", depending on variety. Thrives in partial shade and enriched soil, but tolerates full sun. Needs some moisture. Start indoors under lights six weeks before last frost date in your area. Surface sow and gently press seeds into moist planting medium. Do not cover seeds, as light is needed for germination. Plant seedlings outdoors after all danger of frost. It is not necessary to deadhead spent flowers for continuous bloom.

❧ *Brachycome iberidifolia* (Swan River daisy)
Soft blue, pink, violet, or white, daisylike flowers. 12–18". Thrives in full sun and ordinary, sandy soil. Resists drought. Start indoors under lights eight weeks before last frost date in your area. Deadhead for continuous bloom. Very effective in mass plantings in borders, planters, and window boxes. Pink- and yellow-flowered forms like 'Strawberry Mousse' and 'Sunshine' are now available from cuttings.

Calendula officinalis (pot marigold)
Yellow, gold, orange, apricot, or cream single or double daisylike blossoms. Medium-green foliage. 12–30" depending on variety. Thrives in full sun and ordinary soil. Needs some moisture. Seedlings

Designer Connie Cross, a yard-sale aficionado, found an old cart and filled it with colorful annuals.

resist early spring cold. Sow seeds in situ about four weeks before you set out your tomatoes in your area. Cover seeds with soil or planting medium according to package directions. For continuous bloom, deadhead throughout the season. Flowers are edible and can be used as garnish in salads. Recommended for the worst seashore conditions. New varieties include 'Pink Surprise' (frilly double orange-apricot with 3" flowers tinged with pink), *C. officinalis* 'Radio' (reintroduced heirloom with quilled orange petals, upright, 2'), and *C. offficinalis* 'Sunshine Flashback' (long bright-yellow petals with red underside, 12–18").

Calliopsis, see *Coreopsis*

Callistephus chinensis (China aster)
Red, pink, purple, blue, or white pomponlike blossoms. Dark-green foliage. 6–30", depending on variety. Flowers are fragrant and will bloom from early summer to late summer and are resistant to deer. Thrives in full sun and enriched soil, but partial shade extends life of individual blooms. Needs some moisture. Start indoors under lights six weeks before last frost date in your area. Cover seeds with soil or planting medium according to package directions. Plant seedlings outdoors after all danger of frost. For continuous bloom, deadhead spent flower stalks. This is one of the most popular of all annuals, especially for fall gardens. Move asters every year; they will not thrive in the same spot two years in a row.

🌿 *Celosia cristata* (cockscomb)

Brilliant red, orange, apricot, yellow, and fuchsia blossoms. Medium-green foliage. 9–24". Thrives in full sun and well-drained, enriched soil. Drought resistant. Sow in situ, after all danger of frost. Thin to about 12" apart. Deadhead regularly to encourage more bloom. Blossoms of varieties in the Plumosa group are feathery. Many gardeners consider *Celosia* garish, and the colors can be overwhelming in a garden. 'Fresh Look' has red or yellow flowers and bright-green leaves, 8–10".

🌿 *Centaurea* (cornflower, bachelor's button)

Blue, pink, white, and maroon thistlelike flowers. Silver-green foliage. 24–30". Thrives in full sun, in ordinary soil. Drought resistant. Seedlings resist early spring cold. Sow seed in situ about four weeks before it is time to set out tomatoes in your area and cover with soil or planting medium according to package directions. For continuous bloom, deadhead spent flower stalks. Cornflower is easy to grow, but if you fail to deadhead after bloom, the plant will bloom itself to death and become unsightly by midsummer. *C. moschata* 'The Bride' is lovely, large, and pure white with a sweet scent. *C. cyanus* 'Black Ball' is a rich chocolate, almost black, reaching 30".

Cineraria maritima, see *Senecio cineraria*

🌿 *Cleome hasslerana* (spider flower)

Large rose, pink, lilac, purple, or white spider-shaped blossoms. Lobed foliage. 3–6'. Thrives in full sun and light, sandy loam. Drought resistant and almost impossible to kill. Flowers from summer to early fall. Seedlings resist early spring cold. Sow seed in the place you wish them to grow about four weeks before it is time to set out tomatoes in your area. Surface sow. Do not cover seeds with soil or planting medium since light is needed for germination. For continuous bloom, deadhead spent flower stalks. Although stems grow tall, they are quite sturdy and rarely need staking. Easy to grow. Cleome self-seeds freely once established The new 'Sparkler' series is a more compact form and good for windy areas. 'Linde Armstrong' has small lavender-pink flowers, 18–24". In areas where deer are plentiful, it is said that they will not eat this plant.

Coleus, see Tropicals & Tender Perennials (page 132)

Consolida ambigua (rocket larkspur, annual delphinium)

Blue, red, white, pink, or purple spikes of florets. Medium-green foliage. 3–4'. Thrives in full sun and enriched soil. Needs some moisture. Seedlings resist early-spring cold. Sow seed in situ as early in spring as ground is workable, or sow in fall, as seeds will winter over nicely but will not germinate in warm weather. Cover seeds with soil or planting medium according to package directions. For continuous bloom, deadhead spent flower stalks. A good substitute for delphiniums, which can be difficult to grow. Self-seeds freely in most areas. Blooms from April to September. A new variety, 'Parisian Pink,' offers rose-pink blossoms with a touch of salmon, 3–5', spring bloomer.

🌿 *Coreopsis basalis/Coreopsis tinctoria*

Yellow, orange, red, maroon, or crimson daisylike blossoms. Medium-green foliage, depending on variety. 8–48". Thrives in full sun, in well-drained soil.

Simplicity itself, the yellow of the center of the cosmos is echoed in the petite melopodium.

Drought resistant. Seedlings resist early-spring cold. Sow seed in situ four weeks before it is time to set out tomatoes in your area. Sow where plants are to bloom as *Coreopsis* resents being transplanted. Where winters are mild (Zones 7–9), sow seed in fall. Cover seeds with soil or planting medium according to package directions. For continuous bloom, deadhead spent flower stalks. Recommended varieties: 'Early Sunrise,' bright yellow, fully double; 'Sunray,' a double gold dwarf; and 'Mayfield Giant Grandiflora,' a bright-yellow single with brown-red. Blooms from early summer to late fall.

Cosmos

Bright clear red, rose, pink, yellow, white, or crimson daisy-shaped blossoms. Feathery foliage. 3–6'. Good for the back of the border. Native to Mexico. Thrives in full sun, in ordinary, well-drained soil. Drought resistant. Sow in situ outdoors, after all danger of frost. Cover seeds with soil or planting medium according to package directions. To encourage branching and thus more flowers, pinch tips of plants when they are 12" high and again when 18" high. For continuous bloom, deadhead spent flower stalks. Do not over-fertilize, which will produce bushy stems but few flowers. Cosmos self-seeds freely once established and attracts birds. Recommended for the worst seashore conditions. A new variety, *C. bipinnatus* 'Psyche White,' has semi-double, pure white 3" blooms, and is 4' tall, heat tolerant, and needs to be staked.

Dianthus (pinks, carnation)

Pinks include annuals, biennials, and perennials. Brilliant scarlet, salmon, white, yellow, pink, or crimson carnation-shaped blossoms on attractive silver-green foliage. 6–36". Thrives in full sun, in ordinary, well-drained soil. Drought resistant. Stokes Seeds recommends freezing seeds for 14 days prior to sowing. Sow in situ after all danger of frost. Cover seeds with soil or planting medium according to package directions. For continuous bloom, deadhead spent flower stalks. Avoid taller varieties, which grow on spindly stems and are not generally satisfactory for windy seaside environments. *Dianthus* require good air circulation, so avoid mulching. Flowers, especially the plumarius types, possess an evocative clove fragrance known to drive gentle persons into frenzies of passion. Try new variety *Dianthus* F1 'Grace Salmon,' dwarf, double, 10", early flowering.

Dyssodia tenuiloba (Dahlberg daisy)

Bright yellow daisylike flowers. 12". Although this is a perennial, it is included here because it is short lived and often grown as an annual. Thrives in full sun, in ordinary, sandy soil. Drought resistant. Start indoors under lights eight weeks before last frost date in your area according to package instructions. Plants take four months to bloom from seed. Flowers from late spring to fall. Deadhead for continuous bloom.

Eschscholtzia californica (California poppy)

Yellow, orange, cream, pink, or soft-rose silky blossoms. Smooth, gray-green foliage. 6–12". Thrives in full sun, in ordinary, sandy soil. Drought resistant. Do not over-water and do not fertilize. Fertilizing promotes foliage growth and fewer flowers. Surface sow outdoors after all danger of frost. Do not cover seeds with soil or planting medium since light is needed for germination. For continuous bloom, deadhead spent blossoms. A nearly indestructible plant for difficult seaside environments.

Gaillardia (blanket flower)

Large red daisylike blossoms with yellow-tipped petals. 18–24". New variety G. *pulchella aureus* 'Yellow Flame' from Environmental Seed Producers is a solid yellow. Thrives in full sun, in ordinary well-drained soil. Drought resistant. Start indoors under lights six weeks before last frost date in your area or sow in situ after all danger of frost. Do not cover seeds with soil or planting medium since some light is needed for germination. There are also perennial varieties. Annual types, however, bloom longer. Flowers from summer to early fall.

Glaucium corniculatum (blackspot hornpoppy)

Large red or yellow poppylike blossoms, often with black centers. Bold green foliage. To 18". Thrives in full sun, in sandy soil. Drought resistant. Sow in situ, ¼" deep, after all danger of frost. For continuous bloom, deadhead spent blossoms. Self-seeds freely once established.

Gypsophila elegans (baby's breath)

Tiny clusters of white or pink blossoms. Medium green lance-shaped foliage. 12–24". Thrives in full sun, in ordinary soil. Drought resistant. Sow outdoors after all danger of frost. Barely cover seeds, as some light is necessary for germination. It blooms

Two fragrant plants together: heliotrope and scented geraniums.

just five weeks after germination. G. *paniculata* is the perennial species. Excellent as a backdrop for an annual garden, although some staking will be necessary in windy environments. G. 'Repens' is a dwarf that is perfect for rock gardens and windy conditions.

❦ *Helianthus* (sunflower)
Yellow or white daisy-shaped blossoms. Medium-green foliage. Suitable dwarf varieties are 12–24". Thrives in full sun, in ordinary soil. Drought resistant. Sow outdoors after all danger of frost. Cover seeds with soil or planting medium according to package directions. For continuous bloom, deadhead spent flower stalks. Use only the lesser known, dwarf varieties for seaside plantings, unless you have a sunny, sheltered area where taller varieties (to 10') won't get knocked over by the wind. New compact variety H. *annuus* 'Pacino Cola' grows to only 12–16" and is perfect for pots.

❦ *Helichrysum* (strawflower)
Daisy-shaped blossoms in a wide range of colors. Medium-green foliage. 1–4'. Thrives in full sun, in ordinary soil. Drought resistant. Start indoors under lights six weeks before last frost date in your

area. Cover seeds with soil or planting medium according to package directions. Plant seedlings outdoors after all danger of frost. Blooms from early spring through fall. Deadheading is not necessary. Stalks of flowers can be dried and used in arrangements.

Heliotropium (heliotrope)
Clusters of deep-purple florets. Compact, bushy, deep-green or bronze foliage. 8–12". Thrives in full sun and enriched soil. Needs some moisture. Start indoors under lights six to eight weeks before last frost date in your area. Cover seeds with soil or planting medium according to package directions. Plant seedlings outdoors after all danger of frost. For continuous bloom, deadhead spent flower stalks. This old-fashioned favorite is highly fragrant, scenting the garden particularly in the evening. Strangely enough, it rarely is grown in American gardens. H. *curassavicum* (seaside heliotrope) is tolerant of salt spray.

Impatiens
Pink, white, coral, salmon, red, magenta, purple, or orange blossoms. Deep-green foliage. Variety of sizes including dwarf (8–10"), medium (10–12"), and tall (24–48"). Thrives in semi- or deep shade in

enriched soil. Needs some moisture. Start indoors under lights six to eight weeks before last frost date in your area. Surface sow. Do not cover seeds with soil or planting medium since light is needed for germination. Plant seedlings outdoors after all danger of frost. It is not necessary to deadhead. The tried-and-true flowering plant for shady areas.

Impatiens balsamina (garden balsam)
Pink, white, coral, red, peach, and lavender spikes of blossoms. Deep-green foliage. 24–36". Thrives in partial shade or deep shade in enriched soil. Needs some moisture. Start indoors under lights six to eight weeks before last frost date in your area. Surface sow. Do not cover seeds with soil or planting medium since light is needed for germination. Plant seedlings outdoors after all danger of frost. It is not necessary to deadhead. Consider planting a camellia-flowered mix, a tall variety, and 'Tom Thumb,' a dwarf (8–12"). A good companion for Impatiens in shady areas. Self-seeds freely in many locations.

Lantana see Tropicals & Tender Perennials (page 132)

Lobelia erinus (edging lobelia)
Intense blue, purple, burgundy, red, or white clusters of blossoms, some with white eyes. Mounded, fragile, medium-green foliage. 4–6". Thrives in partial shade, but will blossom in partial sun, in sandy soil. Needs some moisture. Do not allow to dry out. Start indoors under lights ten to twelve weeks before the last frost date in your area. Surface sow. Do not cover seeds with soil or planting medium since light is needed for germination. Plant seedlings outdoors after all danger of frost. It is not necessary to deadhead. Cascading varieties, such as 'Blue Cascade' are spectacular in hanging baskets. *L. erinus compacta* 'Aqua White' blooms two weeks earlier than other lobelias. *L. erinus* 'Big Blue' with its large flowers blooms until late summer. See Perennials list for other lobelia species.

❦ *Lobularia maritima* (sweet alyssum)
White, rose, or purple florets. Mounded medium-green foliage. 4–8". Flowers are fragrant and attract butterflies and bees. Thrives in full sun or partial shade in well-drained soil. Drought and deer resistant. Surface sow in situ, after all danger of frost. Do not cover seeds with soil or planting medium

since light is needed for germination. Be patient, as germination can be slow. A tough plant ideally suited to a seaside environment. Self-seeds freely once established.

Matthiola incana (stock)
Well-formed spikes of double florets in violet, lavender, rose, red, or white. Handsome medium-green foliage. 10–18". Thrives in full sun and ordinary soil. Needs some moisture. Start indoors under lights six to eight weeks before last frost date in your area. Surface sow. Do not cover seeds with soil or planting medium since light is needed for germination. Plant seedlings outdoors after all danger of frost. For continuous bloom, deadhead spent flower stalks. An old-fashioned, heavily fragrant plant that—like the similar wallflower (*Cheiranthus cheiri*)—is rarely grown in American gardens. Select from dwarf varieties, as taller types must be staked to protect from wind damage.

❦ *Moluccella laevis* (bells of Ireland)
Greenish-yellow spikes of bell-shaped florets. Medium-green foliage. 24–36". Thrives in full sun, in ordinary soil. Drought, deer, and rabbit resistant. Start indoors under lights eight weeks before last frost. Soak the seeds in water overnight. Do not cover seeds with planting medium as the seeds need light to germinate. Plant seedlings outdoors after all danger of frost. It is not necessary to deadhead. Unusual green cup-shaped blossomlike leaves add an exotic touch to the garden.

Nicotiana (tobacco plant)
Predominantly white, but also red, pink, yellow, and purple star-shaped blossoms. Coarse medium-green foliage. 24–48". Thrives in full sun, in ordinary soil. Needs some moisture. Start indoors under lights six weeks before last frost date in your area. Surface sow. Do not cover seeds with soil or planting medium since light is needed for germination. Plant seedlings outdoors after all danger of frost. For continuous bloom, deadhead spent flower stalks. Blooms from early summer to frost. Very fragrant, with a tobacco scent. Some varieties such as *N*. 'Sensation' bloom at night. *N*. 'Domino Salmon Pink' has a dazzling salmon color and is only 12–15" tall. Although it is related to the nightshade family, which tobacco belongs to, you do not smoke the leaves of this plant.

🌿 *Nigella damascena* (love-in-a-mist)

Spidery blue, purple, pink, rose, cream, or white blossoms. Medium-green feathery foliage. To 24". Thrives in full sun, in well-drained soil. Drought resistant. Sow outdoors, in situ, $\frac{1}{16}$" deep, after all danger of frost in the spring or in the autumn. Spring-sown seeds bloom later and extend the season, while autumn-sown seeds get an earlier start. This old favorite has recently been rediscovered by many gardeners. Its blossoms can be dried and used in flower arrangements. *N. damascena* 'Miss Jekyll' is a lovely medium blue, 6–12".

Pelargonium × hortorum (zonal geranium)

This is the standard garden geranium, used around the world to decorate patios. Bright red, pink, or white flowers. Coarse, hairy leaves with rings of color. To 24". Thrives in full sun and ordinary soil. Water during long summer drought. Start indoors under lights six weeks before last frost date in your area according to package instructions, root from cuttings taken from houseplants, or purchase plants. *P. peltatum* (ivy-leafed geranium) is useful in hanging baskets and withstands wind.

Pelargonium zonale (fancy-leaved geranium)

This is a relative of the common and popular bedding geranium (*P. × hortorum*). Full sun. Available in many striking and unusual colors with a tropical look. I like the subtle green with white borders, green on green, and yellow-green leaves of 'Crystal Palace Gem.' For a big splash of color 'Vancouver Centennial' fits the bill. It has a rust-color leaf with bright-yellow edges. Heat tolerant, great for containers as well as in mass plantings underneath taller plants.

Petunia

Scores of colors and combinations of colors of these trumpet-shaped blossoms are available. Flowers are available in single, double smooth, or fuzzy. Great for mass plantings and hanging baskets. Thrives in

Annuals come in an assortment of colors, heights, and textures. This beautiful annual border at Leaming's Run Gardens in New Jersey makes use of all these attributes to the fullest.

full sun, in enriched soil. Needs some moisture. Start indoors under lights eight weeks before last frost date in your area. Surface sow. Do not cover seeds with soil or planting medium since light is needed for germination. Plant seedlings outdoors after all danger of frost. For continuous bloom, it is very important to deadhead spent flower blossoms and stalks. Select heat-resistant varieties for seaside gardens. I recommend the single-flowered F1 hybrids of the variety often called *P. multiflora* in catalogues. Thompson & Morgan offers 'Pink Lady F1' with lovely pink flowers low to the ground. Recommended for the worst seashore conditions.

❧ *Phlox drummondii* (annual phlox)

Buff, white, pink, salmon, red, blue, lavender, or pink clusters of blossoms. Attractive medium-green foliage. 7–12". Dwarf varieties of less than 8" are also available. Thrives in full sun and partial shade in ordinary soil. Drought resistant. Used in mass plantings in borders and beds. Sow seeds in situ outdoors, after all danger of frost. Cover seeds with soil or planting medium according to package directions. For continuous bloom, deadhead spent flower stalks. Easy to grow and available in a wider color range than perennial phlox.

❧ *Portulaca*

Single and double red, pink, yellow, orange, salmon, coral, or white blossoms. Succulent, sprawling foliage. 6". Thrives in full sun, in sandy soil. Drought resistant and recommended for the worst seashore conditions. Grows well in hot and dry areas such as rock gardens, seaside containers, paved surfaces, and over walls. Surface sow outdoors after all danger of frost. Do not cover seeds with soil or planting medium since light is needed for germination. It is not necessary to deadhead. An ideal seaside plant and container plant, as the succulent leaves store water.

Salvia (sage)

Brilliant red, white, purple, salmon, and bicolors. Handsome, dark-green foliage. 12–48", depending on variety. Thrives in full sun, in ordinary soil. Needs some moisture. Surface sow outdoors, after all danger of frost. Do not cover seeds with soil or planting medium since light is needed for germination. When plants are 3–4" high, pinch tops to encourage branching and, thus, more flowers. To rejuvenate bloom, cut back old flowers in midsum-

mer and fertilize. Keep in mind that bright colors can be seen from afar and are good to place at a distance while subtler colors are best closer and in shadier places. *S. farinacea* 'Victoria Blue' is my favorite. Its intense blue is stunning when planted with *S. argentea*, grown for its silver foliage. See Herbs for perennial sage.

Scabiosa (pincushion flower)

Ball-shaped blue, white, rose, pink, salmon, crimson, or lavender blooms. Medium-green foliage. 12–36". Thrives in full sun, in ordinary soil. Needs some moisture but does not like soggy conditions. Tall varieties are good for cut flowers, and dwarfs are best used for bedding. Sow outdoors, in situ, after all danger of frost. Cover seeds with soil or planting medium according to package directions. For continuous bloom, deadhead spent flower stalks. Easy to grow and rarely seen in American gardens.

❧ *Senecio cineraria/Cineraria maritima* (dusty miller)

Grown for its stunning silver foliage. 8–15". Compact, moundlike growth habit, yellow flowers that should be cut to encourage leaf growth. Thrives in full sun, in ordinary well-drained soil. Drought resistant. Start indoors under lights six weeks before last frost. Cover seeds with soil or planting medium according to package directions. Plant seedlings outdoors after all danger of frost. An ideal seaside garden plant, native to a seaside environment and recommended for the worst seashore conditions. Silver foliage can be used effectively to set off blue and pale-yellow flowering plants both in borders and in container plantings.

Tagetes (marigold)

There are four basic types of marigolds. African (30–40"); French (6–16"); Triploids, a cross between French and African; and Single, daisylike blooms on long stems. Gold, yellow, orange, white, or maroon single or double pompon blossoms. Deep-green foliage. 6–48", depending on type. Thrives in full sun, in ordinary soil, but will bloom in partial shade. Needs some moisture. Sow outdoors, after all danger of frost. Cover seeds with soil or planting medium according to package directions. For continuous bloom, deadhead spent flower stalks. Tried and true, easy to grow, a perfect plant for a seaside environment. If vivid oranges and golds are not to your liking, select from recently

*'Peter Pan' zinnias have bloomed well into the summer,
sharing the spotlight with the pyracantha.*

introduced white and cream-colored varieties.
'Sweet Cream' is a wonderful hybrid with large car-
nationlike balls of bloom in a white-cream color.

❧ *Tithonia rotundifolia* (Mexican sunflower)
Large scarlet-orange, yellow-centered dahlialike
blossoms. Medium-green foliage. 4–6'. Thrives in
full sun and in ordinary soil. Drought resistant.
Suitable for background and borders. Surface sow
outdoors, after all danger of frost. Do not cover
seeds with soil or planting medium since light is
needed for germination. For continuous bloom,
deadhead spent flower stalks.

Verbena
Red, pink, lilac, yellow, or white blossoms, often
with white eyes, on large trusses. Medium-green
foliage, often fragrant. Drought resistant, 8–12" but
has a tendency to spread. Allow at least two feet of
space. Thrives in full sun and ordinary soil. Needs
some moisture. Start indoors under lights eight
weeks before last frost date in your area. Cover
seeds with soil or planting medium according to

package directions. Plant seedlings outdoors after
all danger of frost. For continuous bloom, deadhead
spent flower stalks. V. 'Serenity' is great for baskets
as well as a groundcover. V. 'Lanai Bright Pink' and
V. 'Lanai Deep Purple' are among the top picks for
growers' trial gardens.

Zinnia
Blooms come in all colors except blue and range in
size from miniatures to giants. Deep-green foliage.
8–48". Thrives in full sun, in ordinary soil. Needs
some moisture. Sow outdoors after all danger of
frost. Cover seeds with soil or planting medium
according to package directions. For continuous
bloom, deadhead spent flower stalks. When
seedlings are 4" high, pinch tips to encourage
branching and thus, more flowers. Zinnias are prone
to mildew, which can make them look unsightly, but
there is some evidence that light salt spray increases
their resistance. Newly hybridized varieties resist
mildew. Z. 'Magellan' is a compact type, 12–14", with
considerably large double blooms. 'Coral' is an All
American Selections winner for 2005.

Bulbs

Among the greatest pleasures of spring for the gardener are hardy, spring-blooming bulbs, both the "major" varieties—daffodils, tulips, hyacinths, and crocuses—and the often overlooked "minor" varieties—scilla, grape hyacinths, snowdrops, and the charming glory-of-the-snow—as well as irises, lily of the valley, and allium. Of course, if you do not live in or visit your seaside home during the spring, you may decide not to install any spring-blooming plants. There are also summer-blooming bulbs, particularly lilies, to enjoy.

You can plant colorful beds or borders using only bulbs, include bulbs in mixed beds with perennials and annuals, or scatter them on the ground and then just plant them where they have landed, for a natural effect. Many bulbs will naturalize. Their planting requirements are modest. Most want either full sun or partial shade in order to perform well, but they require good drainage to grow properly; bulbs will rot in waterlogged soil. Bulbs are virtually insect and disease free, and a bit of soil preparation at fall planting time and some annual feeding is about all the maintenance that they require. And they reward you with dazzling and glorious displays every year, beginning in late winter.

All spring-blooming bulbs must be planted in the fall. Summer-blooming bulbs, most of which are tender and must be dug in the fall and stored indoors over the winter, should be planted in the spring, after all danger of frost, with the exception of lilies, which are hardy and can be planted in either spring or fall.

When planting bulbs, be sure to use a ruler so that you can properly gauge planting depth and spacing. As a rule, plant bulbs about three times as deep as their diameter. You will also need fertilizer. For many years it was thought that bone meal was essential for bulbs, but experience and research have indicated that it will not make a difference. All-purpose 5-10-5 fertilizer appears to provide all the nutrients bulbs need. Dig a hole twice as deep as the recommended depth for the bulbs you are planting and mix fertilizer with soil at the rate of one tablespoon per square foot, three-quarters of a cup per ten square feet, or four cups per fifty square feet. Replace the soil to the recommended planting level and pat the bottom of the hole gently to provide an even surface. Gently press the bulbs in place with the pointed ends up. Cover them carefully, tamp the soil down lightly, and water thoroughly. If there are dry spells during the fall, be sure to water at least once a week. Spring bulbs can be given a dusting of 5-10-5 fertilizer at the rate of one tablespoon per square foot when they begin to emerge from the ground. Plantings of summer bulbs will benefit from a six-inch mulch to conserve moisture, to keep weeds down, and ultimately to fortify the seaside soil.

After bulbs bloom, remove spent blossoms, but allow the leaves to wither and dry naturally before removing them. If you find the leaves unsightly, tie them up in bundles or hide them by overplanting the area with annuals.

Spring Bulbs

All of these spring-blooming bulbs are hardy as far north as Zone 3, and should be planted in the fall.

Allium (ornamental onion)
True bulbs. Round or flat flower heads and onion-like foliage. Flowers late spring–early summer.

Five Alliums to Try

— *A. caeruleum:* sky blue, 18"

— *A. christophii:* deep purple, 18"

— *A. giganteum:* lavender, 5–6'

— *A. neapolitanum:* white, 12"

— *A. rosenbachianum:* violet, 4–5'

Anemone blanda (anemone, windflower, Grecian windflower)
Rhizomes. Bluish-purple, pink, red, or white daisy-like blossoms. Medium-green, leafy foliage. 4–8".

Allium giganteum *flourish in a perennial border (left).* A. thunbergii *'Ozawa,' a more unusual variety, with its dainty drooping flowers, blooms in the fall along with chrysanthemums.*

Tolerates summer drought but must be kept moist in fall and spring. Plant 4–6" deep, 3–4" apart. Soak rhizomes in room-temperature water for forty-eight hours before planting. The white variety is particularly effective when overplanted with 'Red Riding Hood' tulips. Blooms early/midspring for about four weeks.

Chionodoxa luciliae (glory-of-the-snow)
True bulbs. Blue, pink, or white star-shaped blooms. Spearlike, medium-green foliage. 4–6". Plant 3" deep, 1–3". apart. Easy to grow. Recommended companion plants include forsythia, *Helleborus orientalis*, and witch hazel. *Chionodoxa* multiplies readily into substantial clumps. Flowers early spring.

Convallaria majalis (lily of the valley)
True bulbs. Familiar, bell-shaped, fragrant white or pink blossoms. Broad, medium-green foliage. 8". Plant 3" deep, 3–4" apart. These old-fashioned favorites are very easily grown, charming, and sweetly fragrant. Beyond that, the foliage serves as an excellent, noninvasive groundcover. Varieties include double flowered, pink flowered, and a variegated leaf. Flowers in late spring.

Crocus
Corms. Familiar deep-purple, white, yellow, or lilac goblet-shaped blossoms. Medium-green grasslike foliage. 4–6". Plant 3" deep, 3–6" apart. Good seaside plant. Naturalizes when established. Plant same varieties together for maximum effect. Do not mix. Flowers late winter–early spring.

Five Crocuses to Try

— C. *chrysanthus* 'Blue Bird': outer petals deep violet with white margins, inner petals white

— C. *chrysanthus* 'Cream Beauty': cream-white with dark markings

— C. *chrysanthus* 'Lady Killer': violet-purple with white margin

— C. *chrysanthus* 'White Triumphator': white with blue veins

— C. *tommasinianus* 'Ruby Giant': pale lavender with darker margin

---

Bulbs

Pink hyacinths and blue scilla add a lovely splash of color below my camellia, which has survived many harsh winters on Long Island because it was planted facing south and near a warm chimney.

Eranthis (winter aconite)

Tubers. The most commonly grown species is *E. hyemalis*. Bright-yellow, small, buttercuplike blossoms on 2–4" medium-green clusters of foliage. Soak in tepid water for twenty-four hours before planting. Plant 2" deep, 3–4" apart, as soon as they are available in late summer. The most common cause of failure is late planting: the longer tubers sit, the drier they get, and the less likely they are to grow. Along with *Galanthus* (snowdrops), the earliest of all the spring-blooming bulbs, Eranthis often grows right through snow. If conditions are right, they will self-sow and naturalize. Its electric yellow is stunning with the dainty white of *Galanthus*. Flowers in late winter.

Fritillaria imperialis (crown imperial)

True bulbs. Red, orange, or yellow clusters of blossoms. Erect clusters of straplike foliage. 30–48". Plant 8" deep, 8–12" apart. The blossoms do not smell pleasant, so are best kept away from dooryards or windows. Disliked by all animals. Does best in sheltered areas. Flowers in midspring.

Fritillaria meleagris (guinea hen flower)

True bulbs. Purple-and-white or white drooping, bell-shaped blossoms, with checkered pattern. Grasslike foliage. 12". Plant 3–4" deep, 2" apart. Plants often naturalize once established. Flowers in midspring for 2–3 weeks.

Fritillaria michailovskyi (Michael's flower)

True bulbs. Bronze-maroon, yellow-edged, bell-shaped blossoms. Straplike foliage. 8–12". Plant 3–4" deep, 3–4" apart. This charming and interesting species has only recently become available through mail-order nurseries in the United States and Canada. Excellent for shaded rock gardens. Flowers in midspring.

Galanthus (snowdrop)

True bulbs. Translucent, white, bell-shaped blossoms. Slender medium-green foliage. Plant 2–3" deep, 2–3" apart. Along with *Eranthis*, the earliest blooming of all spring bulbs. Once planted, leave them where they are, and each year the display will become more lush and dramatic. A welcome sight in late winter–early spring.

Hyacinthus orientalis (Dutch hyacinth)

True bulbs. More than sixty cultivars available. Blue, purple, red, pink, yellow, cream, white, or orange-peach columnar spikes of flowerlets. Jade-green, straplike foliage. 8–12". Plant 5" apart, 6" deep. Familiar to all, hyacinths are easily grown in the garden. Their stiff appearance make it difficult to imagine using them effectively in most landscapes, but, after the first year of bloom, the stalks of flowerlets loosen up substantially, taking on a lovely, informal look. Their scent is unforgettable. Plant with midseason tulips. Pinks are very effective along with blues. Flowers in early/midspring.

Galanthus (snowdrop) heralds the beginning of spring.

Iris danfordiae

True bulbs. Canary yellow blossoms with grasslike foliage. 6". Plant 3–4" deep, 3–4" apart. Although they rarely bloom a second year, these are worth the effort of planting every fall. Along with *I. reticulata*, they provide sparkling, late-winter color, blooming after snowdrops but before Dutch crocus.

Iris reticulata

True bulbs. Varous shades of blue, lavender, or purple, iris-shaped blossoms. Grasslike foliage. 6". Plant 3–4" deep, 3–4" apart. This low-growing iris often blooms as early as late February. Coupled with *I. danfordiae*'s bright-yellow blossoms, it certainly helps ease the late-winter doldrums. 'Harmony,' deep sky blue, and 'Natascha,' ice-blue and white with patches of gold, are particularly beautiful.

Iris, rhizomatous, see Perennials

Muscari armeniacum (grape hyacinth)

True bulbs. Bright blue, pale blue, or white clusters of blossoms. Sprawling, straplike foliage. 4–12". Plant 3" deep, 3" apart. Most flowers of these charming bulbs resemble bunches of grapes. They perfume the surrounding air with a lovely, subtle, sweet fragrance. M. 'Valerie Finnis,' named after a good friend of mine, Lady Scott, is a lovely powder blue. Flowers in midspring.

---

5 Muscari to Try

- → M. *armeniacum*: blue clusters, 4–8"
- → M. *armeniacum* 'Blue Spike': double blue clusters, 10–12"
- → M. *botryoides* 'Album': white clusters, 4–8"
- → M. *comosum* 'Plumosum' (feather): reddish-purple featherlike plumes, 6–8"
- → M. *latifolium*: rich blue clusters, 10–12"

Narcissus (daffodil)

True bulbs. White, yellow, gold, orange, apricot, and combinations thereof. There are eleven basic types of narcissus according to a system established by the Royal Horticultural Society of Great Britain and followed by bulb growers throughout the world. Shapes include the familiar trumpet, small-cupped, large-cupped, double, and so forth. All grow on erect 12–24" stems over swordlike medium-green foliage. Plant 8" deep, 6–8" apart, depending on bulb size. Daffodils are probably the most universally grown and loved of all spring-flowering bulbs, for practical as well as aesthetic reasons: they are not only pest and disease free, but rodent proof as well. Most varieties perform well for years. After about three years, some form thick clumps of foliage but produce fewer flowers. If that happens, dig them after foliage withers, separate the bulbs and replant. Flowers in midspring.

---

9 Daffodils to Try

- → 'Arctic Gold': yellow, 18"
- → 'Barrett Browning': white and deep orange-red, 20"
- → 'February Gold': bright yellow and yellow, 10"
- → 'Flower Record': white and white-orange, 18"
- → 'Fortune': yellow and orange, 18"
- → 'Ice Follies': white with pale yellow, 18"
- → 'Spellbinder': yellow and white, 20"
- → 'Tahiti': yellow and orange-red, 18"
- → 'Thalia': pure white, 15"

Narcissus (miniature daffodil)

True bulbs. Yellow, orange, white, and combinations thereof. Trumpet-shaped or double blossoms on 6–14" stalks, over medium-green, spearlike foliage. Plant 4–6" deep, 4–6" apart. These mini versions of standard daffodils add great charm to dooryard gardens, rockeries, and foundation plantings. Still, many gardeners have not yet discovered them. They are very reasonably priced and are a joy to behold in the spring. Flowers in midspring.

---

6 Miniature Daffodils to Try

- → 'Baby Moon': buttercup yellow, 9"
- → 'Gold Drops': yellow and white, 10"
- → 'Jack Snipe': white and yellow, 8"
- → 'Rip Van Winkle': double clear yellow, 6"
- → 'Suzy': yellow and orange, 14"
- → 'Tete-a-Tete': yellow, 8"

Among the first splashes of color in this bayfront garden are early tulips, snowdrops, and pansies.

Puschkinia (striped squill)

True bulbs. Bluish white or white clusters of ½–1" blossoms on 4–8" stalks over straplike foliage. Plant 3" deep, 2–3" apart. Plant ten bulbs per square foot. It will self-sow and naturalize if conditions are favorable. This bulb should be more popular. It is ideal for the spring rock garden, or under trees and shrubs. Flowers in early spring.

Scilla hispanica (Spanish bluebell, wood hyacinth)

True bulbs. Blue, white, or pink spiked clusters of 1" bell-shaped blossoms on 12–16" stalks over medium-green, straplike foliage. Plant 3–4" deep, 6–8" apart. These are the tallest growing scillas and also the last to bloom (midspring). Ideal for naturalizing in areas of partial shade or in woodland gardens. I prefer the blue or white varieties to the pink, which looks washed out when in bloom.

Scilla siberica/Scilla tubergeniana (squill)

True bulbs. Brilliant blue, pale blue, lilac pink, or white, bell-shaped or star-shaped blossoms on 3–6" stems over straplike leaves. Plant 3" deep, 3–4" apart. With sensationally beautiful electric blue blossoms. Great for naturalizing and very hardy. *Scilla siberica* is perhaps my favorite early spring-blooming bulb. The blossoms of *Scilla tubergeniana* are pale blue or white. While charming, they do not have the visual impact of the sibericas.

Tulipa (tulip)

In Holland, and indeed throughout Europe, most gardeners treat tulips as annuals; that is, they plant them in fall and dig them up and throw them away after bloom. They do this because they know that most tulips produce fewer and fewer blooms with each passing year. Here in America, however, we tend to think in terms of permanent perennial plantings, so we plant tulips and wonder why they no longer produce spectacular bloom several years down the line.

Some varieties are more apt to provide a continuing display year after year. Species tulips, most of which are the earliest to bloom and the closest genetically to the original wild tulips, will perform the best. *T. kaufmanniana, T. fosteriana* (emperor tulips), some triumph tulips, and *T. greigii* all tend to perennialize and multiply, providing beautiful displays year in and year out. The spectacular Darwin hybrids—a cross between *T. fosteriana* and the Darwin tulip—also may perennialize if conditions are favorable.

There are a number of classifications of tulips beyond those listed here. If you select from each category, you can have around two months of tulip bloom. In a seaside environment, treat them as annuals, digging and discarding them after bloom. Install new plantings each fall. Here are the various classifications according to bloom time:

Early spring: Single early, Double early.

Midspring: Mendel, Triumph, Darwin hybrid, Double peony, Viridiflora.

Late spring: Darwin, Lily-flowered, Cottage, Rembrandt, Parrot, Double late.

T. fosteriana (emperor tulip)

Red, pink, yellow, white, orange and combinations thereof. 4", turban-shaped blossoms on 12–20" stems over medium-green or medium-green and purple, broad-leafed foliage. Plant 6" deep, 4–6" apart. These early-blooming, tall tulips tend to perennialize. Until recently only solid colors were available, but each year, hybridizers are creating new and interesting varieties that are being offered to gardeners. Flower in early/midspring.

---

5 Fosteriana Tulips to Try

- → 'Easter Parade': carmine-rose, yellow inside, 16"

- → 'Orange Emperor': buttery orange, 16"

- → 'Princeps': bright red, 16"

- → 'Red Emperor' ('Madame Lefeber'): scarlet, 16"

- → 'White Emperor' ('Purissima'): white, 16"

T. greigii

Orange, red, yellow, gold, cream pink, ivory, and combinations thereof. Tulip-shaped and water-lily shaped blossoms on 6–16" erect stems over medium green foliage usually mottled with purple or brown. Plant 6" deep, 3–6" apart. Generally larger than *T. kaufmanniana*. They flower after Fosteriana tulips, Kaufmanniana tulips, and some of the species tulips, but before all others. Good for rock gardens and containers.

---

5 Greigii Tulips to Try

- → 'Cape Cod': orange-red, yellow inside, 12–14"

- → 'Oriental Splendor': lemon-edged carmine red, 20"

- → 'Plaisir': cream-edged carmine red, 12"

- → 'Red Riding Hood': brilliant scarlet, 6–8"

- → 'Royal Splendor': scarlet, 20"

T. kaufmanniana

Salmon, scarlet, yellow, cream, apricot, orange and combinations thereof. Tulip-shaped and water-lily shaped blossoms on 4–12" erect stems over medium- green, medium-green and burgundy, or medium-green and white foliage. Plant 6" deep, 3–6" apart. These are much lower growing than the Dutch hybrids and Darwins, but are well suited to seaside gardens. Flower in early/mid spring.

---

5 Kaufmanniana Tulips to Try

- → 'Ancilla': pink and white, 6"

- → 'Heart's Delight': carmine and rose, 10"

- → 'Kaufmanniana': cream with yellow center, 6"

- → 'Shakespeare': salmon-orange-apricot, 6–8"

- → 'Waterlily': cream and carmine, 7"

Tulipa 'China Pink' and bleeding heart

T. species

Yellow, white, red, rose, purple, or combinations thereof. 1–2", tulip-shaped blossoms on erect 3–18" stems over broad, medium-green foliage, some twisted. Plant 3–4" deep, 3–4" apart. If these irresistible, early-blooming miniature tulips are happy, they will multiply as they do in nature. It is certainly worth trying them to see if they become established. Red Batalinii tulip 'Red Hunter,' a new variety introduced by the Royal Horticultural Society, only 8" tall, is great for rock gardens and also as a groundcover. Flower in early/midspring.

5 Species Tulips to Try

— *T. bakeri* 'Lilac Wonder': lilac and yellow, 12"

— *T. clusiana* (lady tulip, peppermint tulip): rose and white, 8"

— *T. dasystemon* (*T. tarda*): yellow and white, 3–6"

— *T. praestans*: pale red, 12–18"

— *T. turkestanica*: white with yellow center, 8"

Summer Bulbs

Except for lilies, the following bulbs are tender and must be planted not in the fall, but in the spring, after all danger of frost. They must be dug in the fall, after foliage has withered or been killed by frost, dried, cleaned, and then stored over the winter in dry peat moss or vermiculite in a cool, dry, dark place. They can be replanted in the spring. Treat lilies like hardy perennials.

Crocosmia (montbretia)
Corms. Yellow, orange, or scarlet 1½" blooms on 24–48" stalks with spearlike, medium-green foliage. Plant in the spring in full sun, in ordinary soil, after all danger of frost, 3" deep, 4" apart. Scratch a light dusting of 5-10-5 fertilizer into the soil when plants emerge and also three or four weeks later. Stake plants when 1' high. North of Zone 7, order and plant new corms each spring.

Lilium (lily)
True bulbs. All colors except blue. Depending on variety, 4–8" star- or trumpet-shaped blossoms, on 2–7' stalks with glossy, dark-green leaves. Plant in full sun to partial shade in enriched soil. Set bulbs 6–8" deep, with small lily bulbs 6" apart and larger (fistsize) bulbs 18" apart. Stake taller varieties as they grow, but be careful not to drive the stake too close to the stalk, as you might injure the bulb. Shorter varieties, such as Hybrid Asiatic lilies, usually do not need staking. Lilies are among the few hardy summer flowering bulbs, and they do not have to be dug in fall and stored indoors over the winter. You can use them in perennial borders and island beds, for masses of color among shrub borders, or incorporated within foundation plantings. A bonus is that lilies attract hummingbirds. These are the available cultivars:

Aurelian hybrids: These are the towering trumpet lilies that can grow to 8'. They look magnificent as a backdrop for a very wide border, but for most seaside plantings they are too tall.

Hybrid Asiatics: These are much more manageable and sensible for the seaside landscape than the Aurelian hybrids, as they grow to between 2' and 4', depending on the variety. The flower spike is compact with many blooms, some in solid colors, others speckled. Be very careful when selecting colors, as some can be quite startling, even garish.

L. speciosum (Japanese lily): Many consider these the most beautiful of all the lilies. Colors are pink, rose, or white, and combinations thereof. Although they can grow to 5', they rarely need staking.

L. lancifolium (Tiger lily): Most of these varieties are spotted, with the petals turned back. Each produces from twelve to twenty flowers per stem. They reach a height of 3–4'. Here again, be careful in your color selection, as some varieties tend to be garish.

Asiatic lilies

Tropicals & Tender Perennials / Containers

Growing tropicals and tender perennials in the landscape has become very much in vogue in recent years. Because of their popularity, these plants have become more accessible through nurseries and catalogues, and increasing numbers of rebellious gardeners and designers are incorporating them into their traditional garden schemes. Tropicals and tender perennials can be grown in containers or planted directly in the ground.

Tropical plants arm the gardener with plenty of ammunition for creative forays in the garden. Their forms are interesting, their colors are extraordinarily vivid, some have fruits that are whimsically bizarre, and many also have unusual textures. If you have the space, and the imagination, you can create a lush, exotic, and over-the-top garden in just one season.

Careful placement of even a single specimen of these plants in your "traditional" garden can dramatically alter its look. Other gardeners use a different approach and create an entire garden of tropical and tender perennials, cleverly including hardy perennials that mimic tropicals to augment the effect. Using colorful ceramic pots and jars and other interesting accessories can further enhance the tropical look. You may even begin to think about painting structures in new colors. Tropical-style gardens are fun! Think bold—in color, size, and combinations. Take traditional, English-style gardening and throw it out the window. Anything goes here.

If space is limited, you can create a tropical look by using containers. Container plantings can transform any deck, patio, or courtyard into a beautiful garden that can be moved or rearranged at will. New technology

Left to right: Xanthosoma sagittifolium *'Chartreuse Giant,'* Cyathea cooperi (*tree fern*), Pachystachys lutea, Colocasia *'Illustris,'* Melampodium paludosum *'Medallion,' and* Ensete ventricosum *'Maurelli' are part of Richard Iversen's splendid Long Island garden.*

has made container gardening easy. With the availability of slow-release fertilizers, your plants can be fed over an extended period. Custom-made soil mixes allow you to grow plants with radically different soil requirements, such as cacti, succulents, and tropicals, right next to each other. New synthetic soil maintains moisture, reducing the frequency of watering, and automatic computerized watering systems will irrigate your garden while you are away—all perfect for weekend gardeners.

Lightweight fiberglass containers are very popular. Moderately priced, they do not crack when left outdoors for the winter, and they come in various styles and textures that mimic bronze and stone or clay. No matter what type of container you use, make sure that it is large enough to accommodate the plants. If it is not large enough, the roots will become matted, and the plant will use up water quickly and suffer during the growing season. As a rule of thumb, choose a container at least three inches wider and deeper than the root ball of the plant, and allow up to six inches for tropical plants and other fast growers. For them, the bigger the pot, the better. Make sure that the pots have enough holes to accommodate heavy rain, and do not fill to the top with soil. Leave enough room to handle downpours.

Keep in mind both where the container will be placed and also the architecture of your house. The style of container is really up to you, but do keep your container plantings in proportion to the size of the area. Create different levels by grouping the smaller pots and placing them in front. Nurseries and catalogues are now offering wonderful container combination kits. They provide you with the plants and a diagram showing where to place them in the pot. Have fun and experiment. After all, that is what gardening is about.

Container plantings of tropical plants, annuals, and small shrubs are limited only by your imagination. Left to right: bird's nest fern and annuals, agave and burro's tail, Chamaecyparis *and burro's tail. Above right:* Ensete ventricosum *'Maurelli' and* Colocasia fallax.

Overwintering Tropicals & Tender Perennials

While many seaside gardeners treat tropicals and tender perennials as annuals, simply discarding them after one season, others find that tropical plants will adapt to indoor life and grow as houseplants in the winter. You can simply dig them up, cut them back when appropriate, wash them to be sure they aren't carrying any destructive insects, pot them, and place them near a southern exposure window. Be sure to keep the environment high in humidity. If the plant is too large to be potted, make cuttings from it, root them, and discard the rest of the plant. When it's time to bring them outdoors in the spring, make sure that you harden them off as you do with seedlings. That is, slowly introduce them to their new environment.

Another way to overwinter plants is to trick them into a state of dormancy by withholding water and keeping them in a dark, cool space such as a garage or basement. If the soil gets too dry, water them just enough to keep them moist. (Once every two to three weeks should be fine in a cool environment.) For plants growing in the ground, simply cut the tops back, dig them up—retaining the root ball—and place them in an appropriate container and follow the directions above. Plants already in containers can be kept there.

Some plants such as hardy bananas require extra care if left in the ground. In areas such as Zone 6, it's not always the cold that kills, but the moisture that creeps through crevices in the plants and leads to fungal attack and rot. Provide the base of these vulnerable plants with some extra mulch in the winter by covering the stems with straw, then tarpaper, and over that, burlap.

Overwintering your tropical plants, especially the larger specimens, does take time and effort, but the rewards are well worth it. You not only save money, and achieve valuable gardening experience, but you also gain a head start in creating your tropical paradise in the spring. A larger plant will grow to greater heights than a smaller plant during that one season of growth.

Since there are so many tropical plants and tender perennials, I will concentrate on a few that are readily available, have a dramatic impact in the garden, are easy to grow, and are not outrageously pricey. For more information see Sources, page 188.

Hardy banana and crape myrtle in tropical splendor at the seaside.

A wonderful layered container planting featuring (top to bottom) datura, coleus, sweet potato vine, and petunias. Above right: Judy Plant used colocasia (elephant's ears) sweet potato vine, coleus, and Mexican feather grass in this container design.

Hardy Palms

Ensete ventricosum (Abyssinian banana)

This is a banana look-alike, 18–36', with leaves up to 10–15' long and over 3' across. Striking looking, with a double-barrel appeal: the front of its leaves are green with reddish edges, and underneath they are a vibrant reddish burgundy. Leaves can withstand strong winds without breaking. Evergreen, hardy in Zones 9–11; root hardy in Zone 8 but must be protected in the winter.

Musa (banana)

Numerous warm-temperate banana species are root hardy in Zone 6 but few do well in Zone 5. They require well-drained, humus-rich soil that should never be allowed to dry out. Fertilize at the time of planting and feed every week afterward. They should be protected from strong winds, as their leaves are fragile. They require some attention, but the effort is well rewarded by spectacular displays of color and form.

M. *basjoo* (Japanese fiber banana) is root hardy to –10° F. In Zones 5–9 it will die to the ground but will regrow. In Zones 9–10 it will remain evergreen and hardy. To 6–14', with slender, bright-green leaves that will grow rather large, up to 6' long. If you are lucky it will produce a beautiful yellow flower followed by green, inedible fruit. This will make a dramatic statement in any garden.

M. *velutina* 'Pink Velvet' grows to produce a flower and clusters of reddish-pink (inedible) fruit all in one season. It reaches 6' in height and is Zone 8a hardy.

Rhapidophyllum hystrix (needle palm)

The hardiest of all palms, able to endure 0° F temperatures without any damage to its leaves. Its main attribute is its large deep-green palm-shaped fronds, which can grow as long as five feet. It likes partial sun. Try to keep it away from direct winter sun and wind, and it will do fine. Suitable for Zones 5b–7a.

Sabal minor (dwarf palmetto)

This is also a very hardy palm with very little leaf burn at 0° F. It will survive –20° F with defoliation but will come back because of its underground bud tissue. Unlike most palms this little fellow can be grown in wet soil. It is a bushy low grower that sports greenish-blue rounded fan-shaped fronds that will reach 3–6' in width.

Tender Bulbs

Acidanthera bicolor (Abyssinian gladioli, peacock orchid)

Corms. Creamy white, mahogany-centered, 2" star-shaped blossoms on 18–24" spearlike, medium-green foliage. Plant in full sun or partial shade, in ordinary soil, in spring, after all danger of frost, 3" deep, 4" apart. Scratch a light dusting of 5-10-5 fertilizer into soil when leaves emerge and again three or four weeks later. Stake plants when 18" high. Water during summer drought. If you are north of Zone 6, it is easier to buy new corms, which are quite inexpensive, than to winter corms over. The blossoms exude a heavy, provocative perfume, most pronounced during the torpid heat of midsummer evenings. Flower in late autumn.

Begonia tuberhybrida (tuberous begonia)

Available in upright and trailing types, both single and double flowers, and various form types such as camellia, carnation, cascade, and picotee. Their cheerful colors provide a jolt in an otherwise dingy shady area. Heights for most varieties are 8–12", although some can reach 24".

Plant tubers just below the soil level with hollow side up. Keep them well watered and fertilize regularly. New varieties: B. tuberhybrida F1 series 'Deep Red,' a nonstop series with 4" double-red flowers, B. hybrida 'Braveheart Rose Bicolor,' F1 hybrid, rose and white, both in sun and the shade.

Overwintering: Plants grown in pots can simply be moved indoors and enjoyed as houseplants. Plants from the ground should be dug up after a killing frost. Place tubers in a warm, pro-

A large clump of cannas combines with salvia to make a huge impact in an annual border.

tected area for about two weeks to dry, then bury tubers in vermiculite or sphagnum moss and store in a cool, 45–50° F, area.

Caladium hortulanum (caladium)

This tropical plant is native to South America and is grown for its beautiful foliage. Caladium leaves are white, green, pink, and/or red, with colored veins and contrasting backgrounds and borders. Combining greens and whites in the foreground of a planting produces a cool, soothing effect. Reds and pinks can fill in a void in the back of a garden and can be appreciated from a distance.

Canna (canna lily)

Rhizomes. Red, orange, yellow, pink, cream, white, or bicolored, 4–5" blossoms on 18"–6' spikes over broad, bright green, blue-green, or bronze leaves, depending on variety. Prefer full sun but do well in partial shade. Plant in ordinary soil, in spring, after all danger of frost, ½" deep, 15–18" apart. Scratch a light dusting of 5-10-5 fertilizer into soil every two weeks during growing season. Water during summer drought. Cannas do well in boggy conditions. North of Zone 7, cut the stalks to the ground after they are blackened by frost, dig roots, and dry in an airy, shady, frost-free place for a few days. Store the rhizomes upside down in dry peat moss, perlite, or vermiculite, and replant in the spring. The dwarf varieties (Pfitzer Hybrids, Seven Dwarfs) are the most wind resistant and are generally more in scale with the garden.

Colocasia (elephant ears)

Tuber grown for its tropical-looking foliage. Loves having wet feet and is a fast grower. For a fun project slice off part of root stock and place it in a dish of water near a window and it will grow colorful miniature leaves.

Dahlia

There are thousands of cultivated varieties of dahlias, in nearly every color but brown and true blue. Bloom sizes vary in width from a mere 1" to a whopping 17". There is a wide variety of plant sizes to choose from as well. Heights range from 2' to 20'. You can pick and choose to suit your color scheme or height requirements. Dahlias bloom continuously from the end of July to frost. Plant tubers 6" deep and about 1½" apart. After a killing frost, cut the

Cannas are often grown for their leaf color rather than their blooms although the flowers are very dramatic indeed. Canna 'Tropicana' is glorious as is.

destroyed leaves down to the ground and dig up the tubers. Wash the soil off and dry the tubers in a protected site. Place the dry tubers upside down in vermiculite and store in a dry, 40°–50° F location.

Polianthes tuberosa (tuberose)

Rhizome. White, 2" single or double blossoms on 15–24" stems with medium-green straplike foliage. Plant in full sun in enriched soil in spring after all danger of frost, 3" deep, 6" apart. Scratch a light dusting of 5-10-5 fertilizer into soil after one month after leaves emerge, and every four weeks thereafter. North of Zone 7, order new rhizomes each spring. Although foliage is rangy and blossoms are only mildly attractive, tuberose scent is so captivating that you might wish to consider growing them in pots near your seating area on your deck or porch.

An assortment of coleus. The pink dahlia perfectly repeats the colors of the variegated coleus.

P. tuberosa 'The Pearl' is an exquisite white with double flowers that will go well with peonies, irises, and dahlias.

Tigridia pavonia (tiger flower, Mexican shell flower)
True bulb. White, yellow, orange, scarlet, pink, lilac, buff, and combinations thereof. 5–6" blossoms on 18–30" stems with slightly untidy, spearlike foliage. Plant in full sun or partial shade, in ordinary soil, in spring, after all danger of frost. Use staggered planting times to vary blooming time. Plant 6" deep, 4–6" apart. Scratch a light dusting of 5-10-5 fertilizer into soil once a month during growing season. North of Zone 7, order and plant new bulbs each spring. Although each flower lasts only one day, the many buds on each stalk create a display for many weeks. Flowers in July and August.

Tender Perennials and Shrubs

Alternanthera dentata 'Rubiginosa' (blood leaf)
Annual, burgundy leaf, 13–17", drought tolerant, good groundcover, excellent trailing plant for hanging baskets and urns.

Brugmansia × candida (angel's trumpet)
Shrub grown for its pendulous trumpet-shaped flowers, partial sun to light shade, 6–8" long, can be pruned to grow as a topiary, 8' high. Comes in soft pink, yellow, or white. Has seductive nighttime fragrance, so plant near window or courtyard to maximize the benefit.

Coleus
Grown for colorful foliage in brilliant red, green, mahogany, yellow, white, blue, or rose. To 24". Thrives in partial shade in enriched soil. Needs some moisture. Surface sow outdoors after all danger of frost. Do not cover seeds with soil or planting medium since light is needed for germination. Keep constantly moist until established. Pinching the tops encourages growth from the sides to produce bushier plants. Exotic foliage adds a tropical touch to any garden, new variety 'Kong Rose,' has huge light green leaves with a rose center, 14–16" tall.

Cuphea hyssopifolia (Mexican heather)
Small tender tropical evergreen, 24". Sun to light shade. Colors: pink, purple, and white. Blooms from spring to summer. Works well in containers and in front of formal borders.

Datura cloranthra (angel's trumpets)
Tender perennial, grows rapidly to 5', with pendulous, fluted double flowers up to 10" long in the summer, with a wonderful sweet scent. You can see it open before your eyes in the early evening. Great for pots as well as in the ground. Comes in white, peach, and yellow. Protect in winter. Caution: poisonous if eaten.

Ipomoea batatas (sweet potato vine)
Cultivars in dark purple, chartreuse, and variegated. Blooms all summer long. Useful as a short-term groundcover or to provide a cascading effect in containers. 'Margarita' has chartreuse leaves 8" long and 6" wide and grows to 6–9" in full sun or partial

shade. For contrast, plant with 'Blackie,' a variety with deep purple foliage.

Lantana
Not technically an annual, but a tropical and subtropical plant that can be easily wintered over indoors and is excellent for seaside porches and patios in pots or hanging baskets. Masses of small flowers in white, pink, yellow, or red. Dark-green leathery leaves. Must have lots of sun to flower, but tolerates sandy soil, wind, and salt spray. Water occasionally during summer drought.

Phormium (New Zealand flax)
Grown for its foliage. Leaves are 1–10' long, depending on variety. Vibrant colors make an impact in borders or accents in a container planting. Used in flower arrangements as well. Comes in solid green and red and in mixtures of white and green, and yellow and green, blue-green, and bronze-purple, to name a few. A versatile plant that grows in full sun as well as shade and is not fussy about soil type.

Tibouchina urvilleana (princess flower)
Flowering shrub, 10–15', fast grower with velvety green leaves and beautiful electric-blue flowers. Prefers full sun and wet soil. Excellent as a main feature in a container planting or in the back of a border. Blooms all summer through frost. Hardy in Zones 10–11.

Xanthosoma sagittifolium (elephant ear)
Tender perennial grown from tubers. Shares its common name with *Colocasia* and *Alocasia*. My favorite is 'Chartreuse Giant,' heart-shaped golden yellow leaves, 2' long, stalks, 1–2' tall. Other species include: *X. lindenii (Caladium lindenii)*, arrow-shaped 8–12" leaves; and *X. violaceum* (blue taro), 2' triangular leaves, 2–3' purple stalks.

Dahlias are available in nearly every color and size. They bloom continuously from late July to the first frost.

Perennials

If shrubs, hedges, and trees are the backbone of the landscape, perennial flowering plants are the backbone of a seaside flower garden. They are long-lasting and winter hardy—that is, each fall their stalks wither and die, but they grow again from the roots, or crown, the following spring. (They are "herbaceous" plants, which means that, unlike shrubs and trees, they have almost no woody tissue that survives from season to season.) They tend to bloom for a shorter time than annuals, some in late spring, some in summer, and some in fall. For this reason it is wise to plan carefully when planting perennials.

Perennials can be used in many different ways in a garden. Ambitious gardeners group them in borders (if they form strips between a walk or lawn and a wall) or island beds (if they are open on all sides). This can be a complicated art. Its aim is to achieve a harmonious blend of colors and forms that changes throughout the spring and summer. Perennials can also be used to brighten the landscape after spring-blooming bulbs have finished, to add color to monotonous foundation plantings, to brighten driveways and paths, and to accent garden structures. The cultivars we have included here adapt well to a seaside garden, are generally readily available, and are, to a great extent, pest and disease free. Technically, some of the varieties listed under Grasses and Herbs are perennials, since they are hardy and bear new flowers every year, and as you can see from the photographs in this book, grasses and herbs are important in seaside garden borders and beds, as, indeed, are annuals.

One of the most satisfying ways to expand your garden is to take extra perennial stock from friends, family, and neighbors, since most herbaceous plants must be divided regularly and replanted to maintain vigor. Don't be shy about asking, for every garden begins this way. But avoid just sticking any old plant you have been given in the ground, willy-nilly, without knowing exactly what it is. If you do, the result will most likely turn out to be an unruly hodgepodge of heights, textures, and blossoms, often in clashing colors. If someone does give you unidentified stock, you can always plant it temporarily in a holding garden, where you can watch it grow to maturity and then decide exactly where it will or will not work in thegarden.

Digging wild plants for your garden is not a good idea. It is much better to identify the plant you like and purchase new stock or seeds from a native plant nursery. For years, Long Island gardeners have dug up beautiful specimens of butterfly weed from roadsides, almost always with unfortunate results for the plants (and the natural landscape). Meanwhile, this plant is easy to grow from seed and widely available from nurseries.

All of the plants listed here are hardy to Zone 5 unless noted otherwise.

Opposite: An island planting of hibiscus (rose mallow), sedum, Crocosmia solfatare, *and* Hakonechloa *(Japanese grass) in the Mattituck, Long Island, creekfront garden designed by Judy Plant for Dennis and Diane Harkoff. Above:* Aquilegia *(columbine).*

❦ Achillea (yarrow)
Yellow, white, pink, and red flower clusters on erect talks with fernlike foliage. 24–48". Thrives in ordinary soil in full sun. Drought resistant. Plant outdoors in spring or fall. Flowers are excellent for drying. Recommended for the toughest seashore conditions.

Aconitum (monkshood)
Dark blue or blue-and-white spires of blossoms on 3–4' stalks. Dark, lustrous green leafy foliage. Thrives in enriched soil, in partial shade or full sun. Needs moisture. Plant outdoors in midspring. Plant increases slowly and once established resents being moved. Plant monkshood in combination with Madonna lilies, Shasta daisies, and white phlox. *A. carmichaeli,* the sturdiest, needs less staking and is the last monkshood to bloom. Late summer to fall.

Amsonia tabernaemontana (bluestar)
True-blue clusters of upright or drooping blossoms and delicate, willowlike foliage. 12–36". Thrives in enriched soil, in partial shade or shade. Needs moisture. Plant outdoors in midspring. Blooms in late spring–summer. Cut plants to ground after killing frost. Pruning after bloom helps maintain foliage, which turns brilliant yellow in fall.

Anemone × hybrida (Japanese anemone)
Pink, rose, or white blossoms with yellow centers. Medium-green foliage. 24–48", depending on variety. Thrives in moderately fertile soil, in partial shade or full sun. Needs moisture. Plant outdoors in midspring or fall. Cut plants to ground after killing frost. Because they are late bloomers, Japanese anemones are particularly useful in the garden. Blossoms are delicate in appearance, which is rare for fall-blooming cultivars. Often sold as *A. japonica.* 'Honorine Jobert' is one of the most popular.

❦ Anthemis tinctoria (golden marguerite)
Yellow daisylike blossoms and gray-green, finely cut foliage. 18–24". Thrives in ordinary soil in full sun. Drought resistant. Plant outdoors in midspring or fall. Blooms mid–late summer. Deadhead throughout summer to prolong blooming. Provides masses of flowers during the summer. In Tudor England *Anthemis* was used for lawns, and when it was mowed, its fragrance, similar to chamomile, filled the air.

Aquilegia (columbine)
Delicate, trumpetlike flowers in a full range of colors on delicate, often feathery, fernlike foliage. 12–36". Thrives in enriched soil, in full sun or partial shade. Needs moisture. Plant outdoors in midspring or fall. Cut foliage to ground after killing frost. Delicate blossoms enhance the spring garden. Blue varieties are particularly beautiful. *A. canadensis,* common in rocky areas, is a beautiful reddish shooting star–shaped wildflower. Other recommended varieties: *A. vulgaris, A. alpina, A. pyrenaica, A. glandulosa, A. chrysantha.*

❦ Artemisia (perennial dusty miller)
Grown for silvery gray foliage. 12–36", depending on variety. Thrives in enriched, well-drained, sandy soil in full sun. Drought resistant. Plant outdoors in midspring or late summer. Especially recommended for the seashore are *A. ludoviciana* var. *albula* 'Silver King,' 36", and 'Silver Queen,' 24". *A. stelleriana* (beach wormwood) is a beach species that requires little care, but it self-sows and can be invasive if you do not deadhead. Also see *Artemisia* under Groundcovers (page 157).

Achillea *(yarrow) under a magnificent Russian olive* (Elaeagnus angustifolia).

❦ *Asclepias tuberosa* (orange butterfly weed)

Bright-orange umbels of flowers in midsummer to late summer on bright green foliage. To 24". Thrives in full sun and sandy soil. Drought resistant. Plants are late to break dormancy, so care must be taken not to dig them up mistakenly in spring. *A. incarnata*, a less familiar native, has pink-and-white flowers. Many members of this family are attractive to monarch butterflies. Do not use pesticides near plant.

Astilbe

White, pink, red, rose, peach, or apricot feathery plumes of blossoms on sturdy, medium-green foliage. Height ranges from 8" to 6'. Tolerates a wide range of soil but thrives in enriched acidic soil, in partial shade to full sun. Needs moisture and are heavy feeders. Plant outdoors in midspring or fall. Remove spent blossoms after bloom cycle. Provides soft, feathery texture to the landscape. Shorter versions such as *A. chinensis* 'Pumila' are excellent groundcovers.

❦ *Baptisia australis* (wild blue indigo)

Indigo blue spikes of pealike blossoms over gray-green foliage. 36–60". Thrives in enriched soil, in full sun. Drought resistant. Will grow in partial shade, but requires staking as plant can become rangy. Plant outdoors in midspring or fall. Blooms late spring to early summer.

❦ *Brunnera macrophylla* (forget-me-not)

Sky blue, tiny blossoms on handsome, medium-green, heart-shaped foliage. 12–18". Thrives in moderately fertile soil, in partial or deep shade. Drought resistant. Plant outdoors in midspring or fall. One of the few perennials that will thrive beneath the extensive surface root system of maples. Great alternative to hosta. Blooms in spring.

Chrysanthemum coccineum (painted daisy)

White, pink, or red, and combinations thereof. Medium-green foliage. 12–24". Thrives in moderately fertile soil, in full sun or partial shade. Needs moisture. Plant outdoors in midspring or fall.

Deadhead after bloom to encourage second flowering. Flowers late spring to early summer.

Chrysanthemum maximum (Shasta daisy)
White with yellow-centered single or double blossoms on deep-green, handsome foliage. 12–42". Thrives in moderately fertile soil, in full sun or partial shade. Needs moisture. Plant outdoors in midspring or fall. Deadhead after bloom to encourage second bloom. Flowers for ten weeks beginning in early summer. Some varieties to consider: 'Silver Princess,' 12–15" with white daisies, June–August; 'Snow Lady,' 12–15", May–August; and a new variety, 'Becky's Shasta,' 3–4' with large daisies, May–July.

❦ Chrysanthemum × morifolium (chrysanthemum)
Wide range of colors including yellow, gold, white, rust, orange, red, purple, and lavender. Many blossom shapes, but pompon is perhaps the most readily available. Medium-green compact foliage, depending on variety. 8–36". Thrives in moderately fertile soil, in full sun, but will tolerate partial shade. Drought resistant. Plant outdoors in midspring. Cut back foliage

after killing frost. The following spring, dig plant, divide, discard woody center, and replant divisions. After planting, pinch shoots every three weeks until July 4 to encourage branching and thus more bloom.

Chrysopsis (golden aster)
Yellow, daisylike 2" blossoms. 2–4'. Thrives in sandy soil, in full sun. Drought resistant, withstands intense heat and tolerant of salt spray. Plant outdoors in midspring or fall. Cut back to ground after frost. Butterflies love C. *villosa*, a wildflower that blooms in late summer and fall.

Cimicifuga (bugbane, snakeroot)
Plumelike white flower spikes bloom with slightly unpleasant scent in late summer–fall, over large leaves. 4–5'. Thrives in ordinary soil in sun or partial shade. Drought tolerant. Plant outdoors in midspring or fall. Can be rampantly invasive, spreading wildly by underground stolons. C. *racemosa* is native to the East Coast.

❦ Coreopsis
Yellow and yellow-mahogany-red, daisylike blossoms on medium-green, handsome foliage. 24". Thrives in

Daylilies are available in many colors. Some can be rather garish but in this garden a soft yellow is used to accompany the reddish pink of the astilbe.

poor to ordinary soil, in full sun. Drought resistant. Plant outdoors in midspring or fall. Very easy to grow. If you want lots of carefree yellow flowers, this is a good choice.

Dianthus (pinks)

White, pink, or red, and combinations thereof, single or double carnation-type blossoms on elegant, blue-green or gray-green foliage. 6–20". Thrives in sandy soil, in full sun or partial shade. Drought resistant. Plant outdoors in midspring or fall. Deadhead after bloom to keep plant tidy. Try *D. deltoids*, which forms 6" mats of pink or rose flowers in spring and early summer; *D. gratianopolitanus*, 6–12", which has rose-pink flowers in early summer and blue-green foliage; and *D. barbatus* (sweet William) a biennial or, at best, a short-lived perennial whose seeds can be sown in August for bloom the following year. All pinks offer a lovely clovelike fragrance.

Dicentra spectabilis (bleeding heart)

Pink or white heart-shaped blossoms on graceful, arching stems over medium-green foliage. 12–36". Thrives in moderately fertile soil, in partial shade. Needs moisture. Plant outdoors in spring. Remove branches of spent blossoms after bloom

A truly hardy chrysanthemum, 'Sheffield Pink' can grow to three feet tall. It will bloom for an entire month in the fall and also makes an excellent cut flower.

to keep plant tidy. Foliage withers toward the end of summer, so it's a good idea to overplant with annuals. Blooms with tulips, azaleas, and dogwood. Adds an air of graceful elegance to the spring garden.

Digitalis (foxglove)

All colors except blue. Spikes of pitcher-shaped florets over medium-green rosettes of foliage. 18"–5'. Thrives in ordinary, well-drained soil, in partial shade or full sun. Needs moisture. Since foxglove is a biennial, start outdoors from seed after all danger of frost. Plant will not bloom in the first year, but will winter over and bloom the next. Once it's established, deadhead after bloom and it may flower again. Foxglove is easily grown from seed and may perennialize. Stunning under climbing roses.

Doronicum cordatum (leopard's bane)

An early-blooming perennial used to contrast and soften spring bulb plantings. Yellow, daisylike, blossoms on handsome, deep-green foliage. 20". Thrives in ordinary soil, in full sun or partial shade. Needs moisture. Plant outdoors in midspring or fall. Deadhead after bloom. Plant becomes semidormant after bloom so overplant with annuals in May or

Sweet William and Hybrid Asiatic lilies

June. Cultivar 'Finesse' has large flowers and strong stems, perfect for seaside gardens.

🌿 Echinacea (purple coneflower)

Plum-pink or white, spidery 3" blossoms with orange cone centers on handsome deep-green foliage. 3'. Thrives in sandy soil, in full sun. Drought resistant. Plant outdoors in midspring or fall. Deadhead spent blooms to encourage second bloom. New cultivar, *E. purpurea* 'Kims' Knee High' dwarf, 15–18", drooping purple-pink flowers.

🌿 Echinops (globe thistle)

Steel-blue thistlelike blossoms on large-leafed, gray-green, hirsute foliage. 24–48". Thrives in well-drained soil, in full sun. Drought resistant, sturdy stems. Plant outdoors in midspring or fall. Divide plant only after three years. Recommended cultivars include: 'Blue Glow,' with light-blue flowers, and 'Taplow Blue,' with larger flower heads.

Eryngium

Steel blue, lacy, thistlelike blooms on thorny, hirsute foliage. 12–36". Thrives in ordinary soil, in full sun. Needs moisture. Plant outdoors in midspring or fall. Deadhead after bloom. Taller varieties may need staking. *E. giganteum* 'Miss Wilmott's Ghost,' 40", is worth the effort. *E. maritimum* (sea holly), 12", is naturalized along the East Coast and tolerates sandy soil. Blooms in late summer–fall.

Eupatorium coelestinum (hardy ageratum)

Fluffy pale-purple blossoms resembling annual ageratum on coarse, hairy foliage. 36". Thrives in well-drained soil, in full or partial sun. Needs moisture but does not like soggy soil in winter. Plant outdoors in midspring or fall. Plant benefits from pinching during season. This encourages sturdy branching and eliminates need for staking. *E. maculatum* (joe-pye weed), 2–6', is an East Coast native found in damp areas and preferred by some gardeners to *E. coelestinum*. Blooms in late summer.

Euphorbia epithymoides (cushion spurge)

Bright-yellow, chartreuse, and green clusters of florets and leaves combine over bright-green foliage. 12–18". Blooms in spring. Thrives in ordinary soil, in full sun. Needs moisture. Plant outdoors in midspring or fall. Remove dead foliage after killing frost. Sap of plant is irritating to sensitive skin, causing a mild rash.

🌿 Gaillardia aristata grandiflora (blanket flower)

Yellow, red, or bicolor daisylike blossoms on handsome medium-green foliage. 12–30". Thrives in sandy soil, in full sun. Drought resistant. Plant outdoors in midspring or fall. Will bloom even in drought conditions. Deadhead after bloom to keep plant tidy and to encourage more flowers.

🌿 Gaura lindheimeri

Tubular white flowers with pink tinge on hirsute, gray-green, willowy foliage. 4'. Thrives in enriched sandy soil, in full sun or partial shade. Drought resistant. Plant outdoors in midspring. Easily grown from seed. Deadhead in late summer for second bloom in fall. Second year, when plant is about 1' tall, cut back to 8" to encourage bushy growth.

Gypsophila (baby's breath)

White or pink sprays of tiny flowers on bushlike, graceful plants. 12–24". Thrives in well-drained, fertile, alkaline soil, in full sun. Needs moisture. Plant outdoors in midspring or fall. Remove dead foliage after frost. Baby's breath lends a soft, cloudlike quality to a perennial planting. *G. paniculata* 'Pink Fairy' offers double light-pink flowers over blue-green foliage, 18".

Helianthus tuberosus (Jerusalem artichoke)
A type of sunflower some consider a weed, with pretty yellow flowers in late summer. 8–10'. Full sun to partial shade. Needs water but can tolerate dry spells well. Tubers are edible and contain no starch.

❧ *Heliopsis helianthoides* (oxeye sunflower)
Golden yellow, double, pompon-shaped blossoms on medium-green foliage. 3–4'. Thrives in ordinary soil, in full sun. Drought resistant. Plant outdoors in midspring or fall. Blooms midsummer to fall. Deadhead after bloom to encourage second bloom. The most widely available cultivar is 'Summer Sun,' dark-green foliage and an abundance of yellow flowers. Only 30" tall.

❧ *Hemerocallis* (daylily)
The familiar lily blossoms on 1–4' stems over strap-like medium-green foliage. Thrives in ordinary soil, in full sun or partial shade. Drought resistant. Plant outdoors in midspring or fall. Foolproof and available in hundreds of varieties and colors to suit every landscape. Interesting note: in China and Japan the daylily is grown as a food crop. All parts of the plant are edible. New varieties: 'Distant Galaxy,' pink petals with lavender edges, 20–30", blooms midsummer; 'Solar moonglow,' 24–26", ivory edged in gold, blooms midsummer to late summer.

❧ *Heuchera sanguinea* (coralbells)
Red, pink, or white spikes of small, bell-shaped blossoms over medium-green or variegated foliage. 12–18". Thrives in moderately fertile, dry soil, in full sun or partial shade. Drought resistant. Plant outdoors in midspring or fall. Deadhead after bloom to keep plant tidy. Like baby's breath, the small florets of coralbells are useful for softening the perennial garden. New cultivar: *H.* 'Bronze Beacon,' with bronze-purple foliage.

❧ *Hibiscus moscheutos* (rose mallow)
Flamboyant, pink, white, rose, fire-engine red and combinations thereof. 7–10" blossoms over stunning lobed foliage. 3–6'. Thrives in enriched, well-drained soil, in full sun. Drought resistant. Plant in midspring, not in fall. Rose mallow is really a small shrub, although it is classified as an herbaceous perennial. If you want to make a startling statement in your garden, this plant is for you. *H. moscheutos*

subsp. *palustris* (marsh mallow), native to East Coast bogs, is pink. Blooms from summer to fall. Cultivars: 'Super Rose,' 3', pink; 'Turn of the Century,' 6–8', red and pink; 'Blue River II,' large white flowers.

Hosta (plaintain lily)
White, lilac, or pale lavender delicate blossom spikes on lush foliage in colors ranging from yellow to dark green, gray, and near steel blue, often edged or speckled with white, cream, or yellow. Leaves can be smooth, ribbed, or quilted. 2–36". Hosta will grow in just about any kind of soil and light conditions, but thrives in partial shade in enriched, moist soil. Plant outdoors in midspring or fall. Remove spent blossoms after bloom to keep plant tidy. Hosta is an indispensable foliage plant. I favor 'Honeybells' (*H. plantaginea* × *H. lancifolia*), which has a light, pleasing scent. 'Dorset Blue' grows to 8" and is a lovely pale blue; 'Great Expectations' has large yellow leaves bordered in blue or green and grows to 30".

Iris, rhizomatous
Rhizomatous irises, which included both Bearded and Beardless irises, are among the easiest perennials to grow as long as you keep the rhizome firm and healthy. The best approach is to provide them with good drainage while keeping the feeder roots below moist but not wet. They come in colors of all shades of the rainbow, and many are perfectly adapted to seaside use. Bearded irises come in many different categories based on stem height (4–40") and season of bloom (early spring–summer). There are hundreds of Beardless varieties, the most popular being Siberians (clumps 1–4' tall that often bloom late spring–summer), Japanese (3–4'), and Louisianas (4–5'). Plant the taller ones in a sheltered area away from the wind, and remember that they need be staked in any garden, seaside or not. The shorter varieties don't have that problem, but do not have the same impact.

Iris kaempferi (Japanese iris): The most spectacular iris. Blue, purple, white, or yellow, and combinations thereof. Spear-shaped, medium-green foliage. To 24". Thrives in wet soil, in full sun, but will tolerate partial shade. Plant outdoors in spring or fall. Many cultivars available. The closely related *I. laevigata* is a true bog plant and may perform even better in very wet soils. Adapts to wetland conditions.

Some recommended cultivars: 'Agoga-Kujyo,' deep purple; 'Aichi-No-Kagayaki,' yellow, 'Thunder & Lightning,' white with purple veins. Blooms about a month after tall bearded iris.

Iris pseudacorus (yellow flag iris): Light yellow to orange flowers over spear-shaped, medium-green foliage. To 5'. Naturalized on the East Coast and found in wet areas. Thrives in full sun, but will tolerate partial shade. Plant outdoors in spring or fall. Various cultivars available. Adapts to wetland conditions. Can be invasive. Blooms from late spring to summer.

Iris siberica (Siberian iris): Blue, purple, white, or yellow, and combinations thereof. Spear-shaped, medium-green foliage. 18–36". Thrives in well-drained ordinary soil, in full sun, but will tolerate partial shade. Drought resistant. Plant outdoors in midspring or fall. Do not deadhead spent stalks, as dried pods are attractive in a fall garden. Siberian iris cultivars to consider are: 'Little White,' white, dwarf in height; 'Fairy Dawn,' pale lavender pink; 'Steve Varner,' sky blue.

Iris, tall bearded: The familiar bearded iris comes in a remarkable array of colors and heights. Foliage is jade-green, spearlike, and remains attractive throughout season. Thrives in enriched, well-drained soil, in full sun, but will tolerate partial shade. Drought resistant. Midsummer is the best time to plant bearded irises, but the fall will do. Remove spent stalks after bloom. Divide and

Hosta (*left to right*) 'Heritage,' 'Big Daddy,' and 'Sum and Substance' with a river birch in the back.

Thalicrum *and gooseneck loosestrife* (Lysimachia clethroides)

replant every 3–5 years, depending on vigor of plant.

❦ *Kniphofia* (torch flower)
Red and yellow pokerlike blooms over gray-green, grasslike foliage. 18–36". Thrives in well-drained or sandy soil, in full sun. Drought resistant. Plant outdoors in midspring. Deadhead through season and shear foliage when it becomes rangy. Torch flower adds a tropical touch to the seaside garden. Some recommended cultivars are: 'Earliest of All,' 18–24", orange, red, yellow, early summer; 'Alcazar,' 36–48", bright red, early summer; and 'Pfitzeri' 36", orange, red, late summer.

❦ *Limonium latifolium* (sea lavender, statice)
Sprays of tiny lavender blossoms on spreading, silvery foliage. 24–36". Resembles baby's breath. Thrives in well-drained, ordinary soil, in full sun. Drought resistant. Plant outdoors in midspring.

Easy to grow from seed. Since it has a long tap root, don't disturb established plantings. Stems are weak so need support.

❦ *Linum* (flax)
Sky blue or white small blossoms on willowy stems. 12–24". Thrives in enriched, well-drained, soil, in full sun and does not like wet soil. Drought resistant. Plant outdoors in midspring. Easy to grow from seed. Grows from last year's growth so make sure old wood is dead before cutting back. Sow in situ in midspring. Thin to 6" apart when seedlings are established. Blooms spring–summer.

❦ *Lychnis coronaria* (rose campion)
Cerise or white blossoms on silver-gray, wooly textured foliage. 24–36". Thrives in ordinary soil, in full sun. Drought resistant. Plant outdoors in midspring or fall. Deadhead after bloom to encourage new flowers, but do not cut back prematurely, as it needs to drop seeds to complete cycle. Additional varieties include: 'Alba,' solid white flowers; 'Angel Blush,' white with a pink center.

❦ *Lythrum salicaria* 'Morden's Pink' (loosestrife)
Tall spikes of purple or pink flowers on large bushes. 30–48". Thrives in ordinary soil, in full sun or partial shade. Drought resistant. Since loosestrife can be invasive and is widely naturalized along the East Coast, causing much damage, please use *L. salicaria* 'Morden's Pink,' a sterile variety that flowers all summer long.

❦ *Malva moschata* (musk mallow, marsh mallow)
Five-petaled, flamboyant, pink, white, or red blossoms. 24–36". Thrives in alkaline soil, in full sun or partial shade. Drought resistant. It reseeds profusely and can become a nuisance unless unwanted seedlings are removed. Cut back plant to the ground when flowering is almost over and you will get a second bloom in the fall.

Monarda (bee balm, bergamot, Oswego tea)
Red, white, purple, or pink. 3" whorls of petals on medium-green foliage. 24–48". Thrives in ordinary soil, in full sun or partial shade. Needs moisture. Plant outdoors in midspring or fall. Deadhead after bloom. *Monarda* is subject to mildew, so plant in area with good air circulation. Try these cultivars:

Astilbe thunbergii, Malva moschata 'Alba,' Lythrum salicaria 'Morden's Pink,' Ajuga reptans 'Burgundy Glow,' Sedum 'Rosy Glow' and Geranium sanguineum var. prostratum.

Montauk daisies bloom in the fall with the ornamental grasses. According to local lore, plants were washed up on the shores of Long Island many years ago when a ship carrying them from Japan sank off the coast.

M. 'Beauty of Cobham,' pale pink. A new one from Holland, 'Fantasy Monarda,' has yellow flowers surrounded by dark pink bracts, 24–28", blooms midsummer to fall.

❦ Nipponanthemum nipponicum (Montauk daisy)

Originally called Nippon daisy. White blossoms with greenish-yellow centers on with deep-green lustrous foliage. 3–5'. Thrives in ordinary, well-drained soil, in full sun to partial shade. Drought resistant. Plant outdoors in midspring. This is a fall-blooming perennial, and, as with all chrysanthemums, bloom must be thwarted for full effect. Shear entire plant to 12" every two weeks starting in June. Do not shear after mid-August. A great favorite in Long Island seaside gardens. Recommended for the worst seashore conditions.

❦ Oenothera tetragona (evening primrose)

Yellow, buttercup-like blossoms on elegant, medium-green foliage sometimes tinged with red. 12–24". Thrives in well-drained, sandy soil, in full sun. Drought resistant. Plant in midspring. Spreads rapidly, but can be contained. Try O. fruticosa, fire-red stalks with green leaves and bright-yellow flowers; and a new one, O. 'African Sun,' with 6" foliage and dainty golden flowers all summer long. Useful as a low border plant or ground-

cover. Vigorous grower, very drought tolerant once established.

Paeonia (peony)

Pink, coral, white, burgundy, red, yellow, and combinations thereof. Single or double pompon blossoms on lustrous, dark-green foliage that remains attractive throughout the season. Thrives in enriched soil, in full sun. 24–48". Needs moisture. Plant outdoors in August or early September. Deadhead after bloom. Cut foliage to ground after killing frost, as disease can be harbored in foliage over winter. Some fragrant varieties are: 'Mme de Verneville,' 'M Jules Elie,' and 'James Pillow.' Blooms in mid–late spring.

❦ Papaver orientale (oriental poppy)

White, scarlet, orange, pink, or peach, and combinations thereof. Large cup-shaped blossoms. 24–36". Thrives in ordinary soil, in full sun. Drought resistant. Has long tap root so does not like to be moved. Plant outdoors in early spring or fall. Remove foliage when it dries during midsummer. Plant goes dormant after flowering, so summer drought is rarely a problem. Overplant with annuals after bloom to cover the bare spot in the garden. I especially like the salmon-colored poppies such as 'Carneum,' and 'Louise.' Blooms late spring–early summer.

Perovskia (Russian sage)

Powder-blue spikes of tiny blossoms on delicate gray foliage, 3–4'. Thrives in enriched, well-drained soil, in full sun. Drought resistant. Plant outdoors in early spring. Cut back to 6" in early spring. Practically indestructible. Flowers summer–fall.

Phlox paniculata (perennial phlox)

White, pink, purple, red, lavender, or orange, often with contrasting eye. Large flower heads composed of individual florets on stiff stalks with medium-green foliage. 4'. Thrives in enriched soil, in full sun but tolerates partial shade. Drought resistant. Plant outdoors in midspring or fall. Deadhead after bloom. Cut foliage to ground after killing frost. Phlox is subject to mildew, so plant in an area with good air circulation. Consider new varieties that are less prone to mildew. *P. paniculata* 'Volcano' is compact, with many branches, and very floriferous. Blooms in summer.

Platycodon (balloon flower)

Purple, white, or pink, balloon-shaped blossoms in spikes over medium-green foliage. 12–30". Thrives in enriched soil, in full sun, but tolerates partial shade. Needs moisture. Plant outdoors in midspring or fall. Deadhead after bloom to encourage more flowers. Balloon flower is difficult to transplant because of its long taproot, but can be propagated from seed. Very dependable once established. Try this new one, *P.* 'Astra Pink,' 6" tall with 3" flowers, blooms late spring to fall.

Goldenrod is native to the mid-Atlantic coast.

❦ Rudbeckia (coneflower)

Gold, yellow, or rust-colored daisylike blossoms on medium-green foliage. 2–5'. Thrives in ordinary soil, in full sun. Drought resistant. Plant outdoors in midspring or fall. Deadhead after bloom to encourage new flowers. *R. hirta* is black-eyed Susan. Easy to grow, producing extravagant bloom. *R.* 'Takao,' has a strong stem with golden flowers, good for windy conditions. Blooms in summer, *R. hirta* 'Maya,' a new variety, is the first double-flowering dwarf rudbeckia, 18–20", with strong stems and bright yellow 3½–4½" blooms.

❦ Saponaria officinalis (bouncing bet)

Pink or red clusters of double blossoms. 2–3'. Thrives in well-drained ordinary soil, in full sun. Sprawls all over in rich soil. Drought resistant. Plant anytime during the growing season. If plants get leggy in spring, trim back to encourage bushiness. Blooms early summer to early fall. *S. officinalis* 'Flora Plena' has pale pink double blossoms in late summer, however, it's a spreader so be careful where you plant it.

❦ Solidago (goldenrod)

Golden, plumelike blossoms on medium-green foliage. 2–3'. Thrives in well-drained, ordinary soil, in full sun or part shade. Plant in midspring or sow seeds, in situ, in early spring. *S. sempervirens* (seaside goldenrod) is native to mid-Atlantic beaches and is a good dune binder in conjunction with American beach grass. Select *S. nemoralis, S. canadensis,* or *S. virgaurea* for gardens that are not directly on the ocean. Cultivated variety *S.* 'Crown of Rays,' 2', yellow, forms clumps, flowers mid- and late summer.

❦ Verbena hastata (blue vervain)

Blue flower spikes on coarse foliage. Drought resistant. Most gardeners would consider this native a weed, but it is a good soil binder on dunes, used in conjunction with American beach grass.

❦ Veronica (speedwell)

Blue, lavender, white, or pink spikes or clusters of blossoms on medium-green, lustrous foliage. 2–36". Thrives in well-drained, sandy soil, in full sun, but tolerates partial shade. Drought resistant. Plant outdoors in early spring. Deadhead for repeat bloom. 'Dark Martje,' a dark blue is most popular. Some

Yucca always makes a statement.

new cultivars are: *V.* 'Caroline in Pink,' purple; and *V. longifolia* 'Bing,' light blue.

❦ Yucca

Large, bell-shaped, white or violet tinged blossoms, over rosettes of green or variegated swordlike foliage. 4–6'. Thrives in well-drained, sandy, poor soil, in full sun. Drought resistant and recommended for the worst seashore conditions. For occasional dramatic accents and a tropical look, nothing beats yucca. But use it sparingly. *Y.* 'Karlsruhensis' is the hardiest.

Herbs

Since most herbs are native to the dry areas of the Mediterranean and Middle East, where either sandy or very poor soil is the rule, they are an excellent choice for American seaside gardens. All cultivars included in this list are hardy throughout coastal areas of North America, except for the far northern reaches of Canada, and all are perennial, unless otherwise indicated.

Connie Cross has created a soothing garden in mainly blue, silver, pink, and white. In this grouping, Nepeta, Allium, Digitalis, *and* Artemisia *are the focus.*

Allium sativum (garlic)

Bulb. Hardy, jade-green, spearlike foliage sporting purple clusters of blossoms in midsummer. To 36". Prefers full sun and well-drained soil and is drought resistant, although regular watering during summer drought is advised. Plant bulbs, or even cloves of store-bought garlic, in spring or fall. Elephant garlic—the giant, milder version—is available through mail-order sources. For larger bulbs, remove flower heads. In August, dig bulbs, clean, hang by their necks in dry place out of the sun until foliage is dry. Store bulbs in a refrigerator. Individual cloves can be replanted after digging for the next year's crop. *A. sativum* 'Thermidrome' produces ivory-white cloves in summer.

Allium schoenoprasum (chive)

Rhizome. Medium-green clumps of spearlike foliage sporting clusters of lavender blossoms in spring. 12". Prefers full sun and well-drained soil. Drought resistant. Plant from seed anytime during the growing season. Chive self-seeds, so to avoid unwanted plants, deadhead blossoms after flowering. An easily grown, indispensable kitchen herb, which is being used more and more for decorative landscape purposes. *A. schoenoprasum* 'Forescate' has 24" pretty pink flowers that are edible.

Anethum graveolens (dill)

Annual. Feathery, medium-green foliage sporting seed heads of yellowish blossoms. To 36". Prefers full sun and well-drained soil. Drought resistant. Plant from seed in spring after all danger of frost, and then again every three weeks for successive crops. An easily grown, indispensable kitchen herb. Feathery foliage can be worked into the landscape nicely.

Artemisia dracunculus (French tarragon, little dragon mugwort)

Perennial. Medium-green, glossy foliage. 12–36". Prefers full sun and dry, poor soil and resents water. Drought resistant. Plant in spring after all danger of frost. Carefree once established and handy in the kitchen.

Chamaemelum nobile (chamomile)

Perennial. Low-growing, spreading plant with bright-green, soft-textured foliage. To 6". Small, white-petaled, daisylike blossoms from late spring through summer. Apple-scented foliage. Thrives in sun to partial shade, in well-drained, ordinary soil. Water regularly during prolonged summer drought. A good selection for planting in walkways near the house; stepping on it releases the scent, which will float indoors. Leaves can be dried and used to brew a soothing tea.

Chrysanthemum parthenium (feverfew)

Perennial. Light-green fernlike foliage sporting white, daisylike flowers with yellow centers from midsummer to fall. 18–24". Prefers full sun and sandy soil. Will also tolerate partial shade. Drought resistant. Plant in spring after all danger of frost. If conditions are favorable, feverfew will self-sow prodigiously. Simply pull unwanted plants.

Galium odoratum (sweet woodruff)

Perennial. Narrow, bright-green, aromatic foliage, with small white flowers in late spring and summer. 6–12". Thrives in shade, in enriched soil. Spectacular although brief under flowering trees. Requires regular moisture. Plant in spring after all danger of frost. Dried leaves can be used to flavor white wine. May wine is flavored with this herb.

Hyssopus officinalis (hyssop)

Perennial. Smooth, narrow foliage, carrying small blue-violet blossom spikes in summer and fall. 18–24". Prefers full sun and well-drained light soil and is drought resistant, but regular watering is recommended. Plant seeds, in situ, in spring, after all danger of frost. Self-sows if happy. Pink- and white-flowering varieties are also available.

Lavandula (lavender)

Perennial. Narrow, silvery-gray, foliage, with white, pink, or lavender spikes of tiny blossoms. 6–48". Prefers full sun and ordinary soil. Drought resistant. Plant in spring after all danger of frost, or in fall. Among the varieties recommended for seaside plantings are low-growing varieties of *L. angustifolia*, including 'Hidcote' (12"), 'Munstead' (18"), and 'Compacta' (10"). To keep plant tidy, shear after flowering. *L. multifida* 'Spanish Eyes,' a fern-leaf type, is a new introduction, 18–24", which tolerates heat and is a good container plant.

Mentha (mint)

Perennial. There are many varieties of this familiar herb. Foliage is deep green, jade green, or purplish, with some varieties variegated in cream or yellow. Try M. *piperita citrata* (orange mint). Thrives in full sun and in ordinary soil. Drought and deer resistant. Plant in spring after all danger of frost. Mint can become invasive if happy; to keep it from escaping, plant it in containers sunk into the earth.

🌿 *Nepeta* (catnip, catmint)
Perennial. Tiny, blue, lavender, yellow, or white sprays of tubular blossoms on medium-green foliage. 1–36", depending on variety. Thrives in well-drained, ordinary soil, in full sun. Drought resistant. Plant outdoors anytime during the growing season. *Nepeta* is an ideal border or edging plant for the seaside garden, unless you have a cat. An intoxicated cat can obliterate a plant in no time flat. *N. faassenii*, a smaller version, is almost a groundcover at 12–24", and *N. grandiflora* 'Dawn to Dusk' (pink) is larger, 30–36".

Ocimum basilicum (basil)
Annual. The familiar kitchen herb has foliage in deep green, bronze, or purplish green. 12–36". Prefers full sun and ordinary soil and requires watering throughout the season. Plant in situ, in spring, after all danger of frost. Look for new varieties, some dwarf and moundlike, many with purple or bronze foliage, and use in plantings for color effects. Basil is also an attractive container plant.

Origanum vulgare (oregano)
Perennial. Small, medium-green heart-shaped foliage. 24–30". Some varieties have a sprawling growth habit. Greek oregano (*O. heracleoticum*) is neater, and more pungent, 24". Thrives in full sun and in well-drained, enriched soil and requires water throughout the season. Divide plants every three years to maintain vigor. Related to annual marjoram, *O. majorana*.

Physostegia labiatae (obedient plant)
Mint family, 3–4' tall, grows from creeping rhizomes, sun/partial shade, likes moist soil but tolerates drought well, pink and white flowers, late summer. New varieties are cultivated for shorter forms and more showy flowers including: 'Vivid,' rose-lilac; and 'Rose Queen,' 2', rose.

In the semi-shade garden behind my barn, I planted sweet woodruff with its lovely scent as a groundcover and a white dogwood for height. The Boston ivy covering the fence turns brilliant red in the fall.

Catnip under rugosa roses

🌿 Ruta graveolens (rue)

Shrub. Blue-green foliage on woody plant. Clusters of tiny yellow blossoms in spring. To 36". Thrives in full sun and in poor soil. Drought resistant. Yellow-green flowers bloom from late spring to fall. Plant in spring after all danger of frost. Cut back each spring to encourage bushiness and pinch plant throughout season to encourage branching habit. Foliage, sap, and oil is irritating to skin and can cause a rash.

🌿 Salvia officinalis (sage)

Perennial. Bright-green or deep-burgundy quilted foliage with lovely violet blossoms in tiered clusters in mid- to late spring. To 36". Thrives in full sun and in ordinary soil. Drought resistant. Plant in spring after all danger of frost. Excellent for foliage color accents in borders. Select *S. officinalis* 'Purpurascens' for purplish tones and 'Tricolor' for variegated white, which appears pink since it's tinged with purple.

🌿 Santolina chamaecyparissus (lavender cotton)

Perennial. Silver-gray foliage, sporting miniature golden buttonlike blossoms in early summer. To 18". Prefers full sun and enriched soil. Will also grow in partial shade. Drought resistant. Plant in spring after all danger of frost. Prune each spring to encourage vigorous growth during season. Do not cut to ground in fall, as new foliage grows on old wood. Divide every three years to keep plant vigorous. In colder climates, mulch plants late in the fall and uncover them in early spring. Cultivars worth trying: 'Nana' (compact form) and 'Pretty Carroll,' 24".

🌿 Stachys byzantina (lamb's ears)

Perennial. Low mat of woolly, silvery white foliage. To 6". Grown for its foliage. Prefers full sun and well-drained ordinary soil. Also thrives in partial shade. Drought resistant. Plant in spring after all danger of frost or fall. Divide every two years for more. Can be used either as a groundcover or an accent in beds. Nonflowering cultivar 'Helen von Stein' (Big Ears) has larger leaves; 'Silver Carpet,' also nonflowering, has silver foliage.

🌿 Tanacetum vulgare (tansy)

Perennial. Bright-green fernlike foliage, sporting clusters of brilliant gold buttonlike blossoms in late summer. 24–48". Prefers full sun and ordinary soil. Drought resistant. Plant in spring after all danger of frost. Blooms midsummer. Divide every other year and replant for continuing vigor.

Thymus (thyme)

Perennial. Many varieties of low-growing, matlike plants in bright green and bluish gray, with silver, yellow, or white variegations, sporting tiny flowers in pink, purple, white, or rose, depending on variety. Prefers full sun but will thrive in partial shade and ordinary soil. Drought tolerant, but results are better with regular watering. Deer resistant. Plant in spring after all danger of frost or transplant rooted cuttings throughout the season. Shear each fall to maintain vigor. Recommended varieties include:

T. × citriodorus (lemon thyme): Distinct lemon scent with green foliage and rose-lavender blossoms. 'Aureus' has bright green leaves edged in cream; 'Argenteus' has gray-green leaves edged in white. 4–12".

T. herba-barona (caraway-scented thyme): Narrow foliage with rose-pink blossoms. 2–5".

T. praecox arcticus (mother-of-thyme): Matlike dark green foliage with white or purple blossoms. To 4".

T. pseudolanuginosus (woolly thyme): Matlike gray woolly foliage with pink blossoms. ½".

T. vulgaris (garden thyme): spreading mounds with gray-green leaves. 6–15".

T. vulgaris 'Argenteus' (silver thyme): silver-white variegated foliage. 6–15".

Groundcovers

Unless otherwise noted, all species included are hardy perennials and can be planted in spring or fall.

Sweeps of Ceratostigma plumbaginoides *(plumbago) and* Ajuga *surround a bank of fountain grass.*

Achillea tomentosa (woolly yarrow)
Yellow, tightly structured flower heads on fernlike foliage. 3–6". Thrives in enriched, sandy soil, in full sun. Drought resistant once established. Deadhead spent blooms to encourage repeat bloom. Cultivars worth trying: 'Aurea,' low, compact with yellow flowers; 'Maynard Gold,' bright yellow, 6".

❦ Ajuga (bugleweed)
Blue, purple, or white blossoms on vigorous, semi-evergreen plants with dark-green, burgundy, bronze-purple, or variegated foliage, depending on variety. 4–10". Thrives in ordinary soil, in full sun or partial shade. Drought resistant. If you prefer a less vigorous variety, select A. *genevensis* (Geneva

bugle) or *A. reptans* 'Burgundy Glow,' with variegated foliage of burgundy, green, and cream. Use under shade trees in mass plantings.

Alyssum saxatile, see Aurinia saxatilis

Arabis caucasica (rock cress)
White or rose-pink clusters of blossoms over silver-green tufted foliage. 12". Thrives in ordinary, gritty, well-drained sandy soil in full sun. Requires moisture, but is drought resistant once established. Plant in fall. One of the earliest blooming perennials, well-suited to a rock garden or border as well. New variety *A. caucasica* 'Variegata' has variegated soft white-and-green foliage and white blooms.

Arctostaphylos uva-ursi (bearberry)
A ubiquitous low-growing North American native that sports brilliant red berries and evergreen foliage that turns bronze in fall. Thrives in poor, sandy soil in hot sun. Drought resistant. Particularly attractive and maintenance free. This is the best groundcover for secondary dune areas.

Arenaria verna caespitosa (moss sandwort)
Spring-blooming, white, starlike blossoms on delicate, mosslike foliage, 1–3", thrives in full sun or partial shade in ordinary soil. Drought resistant. Ideal for tucking into wall cracks or between stepping stones.

Armeria maritima (thrift)
White or deep-rose blossoms on semi-evergreen foliage. 4". Thrives in ordinary, sandy soil, in full sun or partial shade. Drought resistant. One of the best groundcovers for seaside gardens. Very easy to propagate. Excellent along stone walkways, rock gardens, and bluffs. *A. maritima* 'Joystick Lilac Shades' has pink to rose to lilac flowers on strong stems.

Aronia melanocarpa, see Shrubs & Trees (page 173)

Artemisia schmidtiana (silver mound)
Grown for its silver foliage. To 12". Thrives in poor, sandy soil in full sun. Drought resistant (resents watering). Foliage adds texture to garden or can be dried and used in arrangements or for Christmas decorations. Excellent groundcover for secondary dune areas. Deer resistant.

Artemisia stelleriana (beach wormwood)
Another silvery plant, with small clusters of yellow blossoms. 6"–24" depending on variety. Native to the East Coast. Thrives in poor, sandy soil in full sun. Drought resistant (resents watering). Excellent groundcover for secondary dune areas.

Aurinia saxatilis (gold dust)
Brilliant sulfur-gold clusters of blossoms in spring, on silvery-gray foliage. 8–10". Thrives in ordinary soil and prefers full sun. Drought resistant. Attracts butterflies and looks good with *Iberis* and *Phlox subulata*. Plant in early spring. Usually sold as *Alyssum saxatile*. 'Citrina' is a pale yellow version, more subtle than the brilliant-yellow varieties.

Calluna vulgaris (heather)
Tiny, white, pink, or red blossoms spikes in summer or fall on evergreen foliage. 18". Thrives in poor soil, in full sun. In partial shade, bloom will be less profuse. Needs some moisture. *C. vulgaris* 'Flamingo', upright, fiery red, purple, blooms August–September. 'October White,' is upright, white, September–October.

Cerastium tomentosum (snow-in-summer)
White blossoms in June on woolly gray foliage. 6–10". Thrives in poor soil and in full sun, and has been known to prosper in pure sand. Drought resistant. Shear after blooming to keep it tidy during summer. Try *C. tomentosum* 'Siver Carpet,' pure white flowers, plant with spring bulbs.

Ceratostigma plumbaginoides (blue plumbago)
Stunning electric-blue blossoms on red stems in late August through late fall on glossy deep-green foliage that turns bronze in cold weather. 6–12". Thrives in full sun or light shade, in ordinary soil. Drought resistant. Can become weedy if not contained. New dwarf version now available.

Cornus canadensis (bunchberry)
Very small greenish blossoms with white bracts in spring on medium-green foliage. 4". Needs moist, organic soil and partial shade. Edible red berries persist through autumn. This North American woodland native is not hardy south of Zone 6.

Cotoneaster, see Shrubs & Trees (page 173)

Erica carnea (spring heath)

Spring-blooming cousin of heather, with red, pink, or white spikes of blossoms on evergreen foliage. 18". Thrives in poor soil, in full sun. In partial shade, bloom will be less profuse. Needs some moisture. *E. carnea* 'Vivellii,' a low, spreading form, has red flowers and deep-green foliage that turns bronze in winter. Plant among white varieties for contrast.

❦ Euonymus fortunei (winter creeper)

Deep-green evergreen foliage with pale-red fruit in summer and fall. Thrives in full sun or partial shade and in poor soil. Drought resistant. Look for low-growing varieties, many of which have variegated foliage in white, pink, or yellow. Can also be used as a climbing vine.

Gaultheria procumbens (wintergreen)

Low, creeping evergreen native with inconspicuous white flowers, often with a touch of pink, in spring followed by scarlet/violet fruits in midsummer on shiny dark-green leaves. 6". Thrives in partial shade and in moist sandy soil. The aromatic leaves were once used to make oil of wintergreen and can be used to brew wintergreen tea. Not hardy south of Zone 7.

Hedera helix (English ivy)

Ivy, always grown for its handsome foliage, which ranges from deep green to yellow or white variegations depending on the variety chosen, can be trained either as a vine or a groundcover. Thrives in ordinary soil, in partial to deep shade, and once established is drought resistant. Great plant to combat soil erosion. Prune every fall to keep in bounds.

Holcus lanatus 'Variegatus,' see Grasses (page 163)

❦ Hypericum calycinum (St. John's wort)

Big bright-yellow blossoms in late summer on medium-green foliage. 6–12". Thrives in full sun and in sandy soil. Drought resistant. Foliage turns purplish in fall. Hardy from Cape Cod south, but somewhat iffy in Maine. Every year or two in the winter mow it to the ground to rejuvenate.

❦ Iberis sempervirens (candytuft)

Clusters of white blossoms on lustrous, needlelike evergreen foliage. 6–24". Thrives in full sun and in ordinary soil. Drought resistant. Many improved varieties now available. The dwarf *I. saxatilis* (rock

English ivy

candytuft) is particularly attractive. Shear back after bloom.

❦ Lamium maculatum (dead nettle)

Clusters of while blossoms on a plant grown mostly for its silvery-white and green variegated foliage. 12". Thrives in light shade and in ordinary soil. Drought resistant. A Long Island favorite is *L. maculatum* 'White Nancy,' green and silver leaves with white flowers. Also try *L. maculatum* 'Shell Pink,' green leaves with silver and pink flowers; and *L. maculatum* 'False Salvia,' dark-green leaves spotted with white, 8".

❦ Leiophyllum buxifolium (sand myrtle)

Native to southeastern coastal areas. Small, waxy white blossoms in May on evergreen foliage. Spreading to 5'. Thrives in full sun and in ordinary soil. Drought resistant. Not all that attractive a plant, but it will survive in secondary dune areas.

❦ Liriope spicata (creeping lilyturf)

Lilac to white blossoms on spikes in mid- to late summer, on green grasslike foliage. 8–12". Thrives in partial shade to shade in ordinary soil. Drought resistant. To propagate, divide in spring and space plants 2–3" apart.

Mitchella repens (partridgeberry)

East Coast woodland native. Small white or pink flowers in late spring followed by red berries, on a creeping groundcover with round, dark-green ever-green leaves, 2". Thrives in partial shade in ordinary soil.

❧ *Opuntia humifusa* (prickly pear)
Surprise! The only native cactus plant hardy in northern climates. Large yellow or orange blossoms on thorny cactus foliage. 5–12". Thrives in full sun and in sandy soil. Bright-yellow showy flowers in late spring and early summer. Drought resistant. Weeding prickly pear can be agony, as the thorns are very sharp and it spreads rampantly. Frequently sold as *O. compressa*.

Pachysandra terminalis
White blossoms in spring on deep glossy green or variegated foliage. Prefers partial shade or deep shade and ordinary soil. Once established it is drought resistant, but prolonged drought will kill it. Propagates easily from cuttings or from unearthed, unwanted stock: just wrap roots around your finger and plant. It is slow to establish, however. When my late mother was young, she had a substantial planting of pachysandra on her property. Neighbors were envious, and so, every several days, she would pull some out, put it in a pail, and deliver it to various neighbors' doors.

Designer Connie Cross used various thymes and heathers in lieu of a lawn not only as groundcovers but for color and scent as well.

As a result she became known as "Notre Dame de Pachysandra."

Paxistima canbyi (cliff green)
Tiny white flowers on evergreen foliage. 12". Thrives in partial shade and in acid soil and requires some moisture. Grow this East Coast native for its magnificent bronze autumn foliage.

Phlox divaricata (wild blue phlox)
Lovely blue or lavender blossoms in spring on medium-green leaf clusters, 10–20". Prefers partial shade and thrives in ordinary soil but needs moisture. Spreading stems put down roots.

Phlox stolonifera (creeping phlox)
Purplish blossoms on mats of foliage in spring. 6–12". Prefers shade and ordinary soil and is drought resistant once established. A native plant that adapts well to seaside environments. *P. stolonifera* 'Bruce's White' has pure-white 8" flowers in spring.

Phlox subulata (moss pink)
Small white, pink, or pale blue clusters of blossoms in midspring, on matlike semi-evergreen foliage. 6". Thrives in full sun or partial shade in ordinary soil. Drought resistant once established. A better choice than *P. stolonifera*, with many new varieties in clear colors available.

Polemonium caeruleum (Jacob's ladder)
Small, cup-shaped blue or white blossoms in mid- to late spring on delicate medium-green mounds of foliage. To 24". Thrives in either sun or shade, in average soil. Drought resistant once established. Plant in spring only. 'Blue Pearl' and 'Album' varieties are recommended.

Rosa wichuraiana, see Roses (page 166)

Sedum (stonecrop)
Scores of varieties with white, pink, yellow, gold, red, or blue blossoms on jade-green, yellow, purple, red, or gray succulent foliage. Prefers full sun and ordinary soil. Drought resistant. Plant at any time during the season. A few varieties are invasive. *S. spectabile* 'Autumn Joy,' the most spectacular cultivar, sports large mauve-pink flower heads that turn brilliant rust in fall on succulent, jade green foliage. To 36". Research into available varieties is well worth the effort, for some (for example, *S. album*, white flowers; *S. kamtchaticum*, yellow flowers) are exquisite.

Sempervivum (hens-and-chickens)
The perfect companion for sedums has elegant rosettes of succulent foliage in reds, greens, browns, and blue-grays. Stalks of bizarre blossoms emerge in early summer. Prefers full sun and ordinary soil. Drought resistant. Research into available varieties is worth the effort. Its only problem is that each rosette flowers only once and then it dies, leaving a gap.

Stachys byzantina, see Herbs (page 152)

Thymus, see Herbs (page 152)

Veronica (speedwell)
There are many varieties of veronica, but only a few can be grown as groundcovers. Most offer purple, white-pink, or blue blossoms on pale-green or deep-green foliage. Prefers full sun and ordinary soil. Drought resistant once established. *V. allioni* has spikes of purple blossoms over leathery deep-green foliage, 4". *V. filiformis*, the familiar lawn pest, with small pale-blue blossoms on dense mats of medium-green foliage, is very invasive. *V.* 'Giles van Hees' is a delightful dwarf with 6" pink spikes. Taller-growing varieties are not appropriate for use as groundcovers.

Vinca minor (periwinkle, creeping myrtle)
This familiar groundcover has medium-blue or white blossoms on attractive glossy green foliage. 6". A very versatile plant in terms of adapting to the environment, it thrives in full sun, partial shade, or deep shade, in ordinary soil. Drought resistant. Can be invasive if conditions are ideal. *V. minor* 'Jekyll's White' has beautiful snow-white flowers; use as a groundcover interplanted with yellow, blue, or pink spring bulbs, or with stepping-slopes to fight soil erosion. A new variety, 'First Kiss Blueberry,' the first violet-blue–flowered vinca has large, 2" blooms, 11" tall.

Ferns

Ferns can be useful in the seaside garden, although they will not thrive in beach or dune environments. Use them in areas farther away from the sea, or where soil has been substantially improved. Most ferns require moisture during the summer drought period. The ferns listed below are deciduous, so you should remove spent foliage after a killing frost. All are hardy to Zone 5.

Maidenhair ferns, azaleas, and rhododendrons.

Farfugium 'Aureomaculatum,' hosta, Japanese painted fern, and tall-growing lady fern light up a shady corner. Left: Ferns thrive in the spray of a waterfall.

Adiantum pedatum (maidenhair fern)
Native fern with lacy, soft green foliage. 18–24". Prefers deep to light shade; rich, moist, well-drained soil; and moisture throughout the growing season. Plant in spring. Does well in pockets near a water garden.

Athyrium filix-femina (lady fern)
Deep-cut, bright yellow-green foliage. 24–48". Prefers partial shade, ordinary soil, and moisture throughout growing season. Does well underneath tall trees. Plant in spring.

Athyrium nipponicum 'Pictum' (Japanese painted fern)
Sometimes known as Athyrium goeringianum pictum. Coarse gray-green and red foliage. 12–18". Prefers partial shade, as sun leaches out color. Needs enriched soil with considerable amounts of organic matter worked in. Plant in spring. Water regularly during growing season.

Matteuccia struthiopteris (ostrich fern)
Yellow-green, feathery fronds. 3–6'. Prefers deep to light shade. Needs enriched soil with considerable amounts of organic matter worked in. Plant in spring. Water regularly during growing season.

Osmunda cinnamomea (cinnamon fern)
Native fern with deep green, waxy textured fronds on cinnamon-colored stalks. 3–48". Slow growing, prefers deep to light shade. Needs enriched soil with considerable amounts of organic matter worked in. Plant in spring. Water regularly during growing season.

Osmunda regalis (royal fern)
Native fern with deep, forest-green fronds. 4–6'. Prefers deep to light shade and slightly acidic soil, grows near springs, bogs, and ponds. Plant in spring. Water regularly during growing season.

Grasses

Bloom times refer to peak time for plumy panicles or seed heads, not for blossoms, as grasses do not sport bloom. All cultivars included are hardy throughout the United States unless otherwise indicated.

❦ *Ammophila breviligulata* (American beach grass)

Open-spreading grass. Native grass with narrow, whiplike leaves. 12". Your first line of defense against beach erosion. Prefers full sun and sandy soil. Drought resistant once established. This vigorous grower can be propagated easily by division of the rootstock. The first grass to plant to stabilize dunes or hold sandy soil. Recommended for the worst seashore conditions.

Cortaderia selloana 'Pumila' (compact pampas grass)

Ornamental grass. Silky panicles on tall bluish clumps. 4–6'. Thrives in full sun in ordinary soil. Provide moisture during extended summer drought until established. Hardy in Zones 5–9. Plant in spring or fall. Cut foliage to ground before spring growth commences.

Festuca (fescue grass)

Ornamental grass for massing. Grows in tufts to 8–12". Fast growing, thrives in ordinary soil. Prefers dry conditions once established, but should be watered regularly during prolonged summer drought as its roots like moisture. Plant in spring. Cut foliage to ground before spring growth commences. Many varieties are available, and some make good groundcovers. F. 'Boulder Blue,' metallic blue, 8"; F. glauca 'Elijah Blue,' rounded tufts of thin blue grass, 8", blooms in the summer.

❦ *Holcus lanatus 'Variegatus'* (variegated velvet grass)

Ornamental grass for massing. A spreading soft-textured grass, green-and-white variegated leaves, 8". Prefers moist soil but tolerates sandy soil. Drought resistant once established. Cut foliage to the ground in late summer or early fall. Can be grown as a groundcover.

Imperata cylindrica rubra (Japanese bloodgrass)

Ornamental open-spreading grass. Erect, pointed foliage with red tips. 12–24". Plant in partial shade for most leaf color. Tolerates poor soil and dry spells but should be watered regularly during prolonged summer drought. Perfect for borders or containers. Plant in spring. Cut foliage to ground before spring growth commences. Not hardy north of Long Island.

163

Sedum and American beach grass

Beach plum and American beach grass

Miscanthus

Ornamental grass. Broad, grassy foliage with silvery-tan plumes in midsummer. 4–7'. Prefers partial shade but tolerates full sun. Plant in ordinary soil. Tolerates dry spells but should be watered regularly during prolonged summer drought. Plant in spring or fall. Cut foliage to ground before spring growth commences. Useful seaside species include M. *saccariflorus* (silver banner grass), M. *sinensis* 'Gracillimus' (maiden grass), and M. *sinensis* 'Zebrinus' (zebra grass).

Muhlenbergia capillaris (gulf muhlygrass)

Clump-forming native grass found in eastern North America, to 3' tall and 3' wide, full sun to light shade, blooms in late summer, non invasive, with beautiful purple haze-like plumes, hardy in Zones 5–10. It is salt-spray tolerant, and grows in poor soils. Excellent as a groundcover in poor soil areas. Also used in borders to provide texture and color.

Panicum virgatum (switch grass)

Ornamental grass. Finely cut green foliage. 4–7'. Delicate cloudlike blooms from midsummer to fall. Prefers full sun and ordinary soil. Water regularly as roots prefer moisture (species is native to eastern salt marshes). Plant in spring or fall. Cut foliage to ground before spring growth commences. Bloom persists through winter and adds interesting touch to winter landscape. Attractive garden varieties with leaves that turn red in the fall ('Rehbraun,' 'Rotstrahlbusch,' 'Rubrum') are not as tall.

Pennisetum alopecuroides (fountain grass)

Ornamental grass. Very fine arching foliage. 3–4'. Rose-tan foxtail-shaped bloom from midsummer through fall. Prefers full sun and sandy soil. Tolerates dry spells, but should be watered regularly during prolonged summer drought. Plant in spring. Cut foliage to ground before spring growth commences. Not hardy north of Long Island.

❧ Phyllostachys (bamboo)

Running bamboo. Mature culms to 30' (15' in confined spaces) sporting fanlike foliage. Thrives in full sun or partial shade and in sandy soil. Tolerates dry spells when established, but should be watered regularly during prolonged summer drought (P. *nigra*, black bamboo, has greater

drought tolerance). Most available varieties are hardy to Zone 7 and some to Zone 5. Dwarfs are also available. *Bambusa multiplex* 'Tiny Fern,' 9' max. height, is hardy to 15° F. Saturate transplanted bamboo daily for ten days. Older culms should be thinned out every autumn after five or six years. To curb spread of established groves, a barrier of sheet metal or concrete should be sunk

Gardening on sand can be difficult, so the gardener chooses plants that are tough and easy to grow. Many of these (with the exception of the hydrangeas) need little water. Russian sage, daylilies, and gazania are in the back, where Max, the dog, stands guard.

24–30" into the ground. Bamboo is a good soil binder and is edible, and the culms are useful for constructing fences and trellises. People either love it or find it terrifying.

🌱 *Uniola paniculata* (sea oats)

Open-spreading grass. Native to southeast coastal United States. Grassy foliage, 2–5'. Thrives in full or partial sun and fertile, moist, sandy soil. Extremely salt tolerant, and a good dune stabilizer. Drought resistant. Plant in spring, and cut back in the winter. Not hardy north of Long Island. Can be established on dunes with American beach grass.

Roses

The world of roses is too large to cover in a brief list, so I recommend that you familiarize yourself with the varieties that thrive in your area. Roses can be used as shrubs, hedges, climbers, and groundcovers, and all need at least six to seven hours of full sun a day. Most require fortified soil and a reasonable amount of care, including watering, feeding, spraying, and pruning, in order to fulfill their potential. The three main classifications of roses are Wild roses, Old Garden roses (often called "old-fashioned roses"), and Modern roses (hybrid tea roses), and each group includes shrub and climbing varieties. Among roses, the shrubs tend to be larger and more sprawling than the stiffer bushes, which are traditionally reserved for planting in beds. Here are some of the types you might encounter in plant catalogues, with some recommendations.

Rosa rugosa *thrives on the sand dunes (above). Right:
'Lavender Lassie' and 'Norwich Pink' roses grow at La
Roseraie in Southampton, New York. The fallen rose
petals possess an ethereal beauty.*

Fairy roses grown as a topiary.

Old Garden Roses

These roses, such as Cabbage, Damask, Gallica, and Alba roses—the pride of nineteenth-century horticulture—are now enjoying a renewed popularity with gardeners. Not only are they intensely fragrant, but their bloom is profuse, most are disease resistant, and some are even drought resistant, making them a good selection for a seaside garden. Unlike hybrids, they offer one seasonal blooming in the spring. Many grow into large, somewhat unruly, plants and they need space to be displayed to their best advantage.

Modern Roses

These large-flowered varieties, formerly called Hybrid Teas, are the best known of all roses. Most are compact bushes, 3–5' tall, that produce single flowers on long stems. Some are fragrant, but many are not. These roses, as a rule, take the most care to grow.

Grandiflora roses, which are produced by crossing large-flowered and cluster-flowered roses, are somewhat larger plants that produce up to a half-dozen blooms on each stem. They are also more vigorous and most are fragrant.

Cluster-flowered roses, formerly called Floribunda roses, are small, 2–4', bushes that are extremely vigorous, hardy, and disease resistant. They are usually covered with blossoms, which are smaller than large-flowered or Grandiflora roses. 'Betty Prior' is a pink cluster-flowered rose that has long been popular in America because it will grow dependably almost anywhere, even on the seashore.

Polyantha roses are low-growing with small flowers in great abundance. Few Polyanthas are of interest today (they were popular in the 1920s), but one worth trying as a groundcover is 'The Fairy,' a virtually indestructible, disease-free plant with pink flowers and glossy green leaves.

Finally, there are English roses, magnificent new hybrids that are the culmination of nearly forty years of research and rose breeding by David Austin of Great Britain. They are the result of crossing Old Garden roses with Modern Bush roses. For form and flower, delicacy of coloring, and rich fragrance, they can be compared with Damask, Gallica, and Alba roses, and they bloom repeatedly throughout the season. Because they are less demanding than other Modern roses, they are a good bet for a seaside garden.

Shrub Roses

There are both Modern and Wild Shrub roses. They grow to 3–5' depending on variety, with white, pink, red, yellow, or orange-toned blossoms. These are tough plants, and when happy, become thick hedges with profuse bloom. Wild Shrub roses, especially *Rosa rugosa*, are a good selection for difficult seaside areas. *R. rugosa* is a marvelous plant that flowers first in late spring on 6' canes with deep-green leathery foliage, and then repeatedly throughout the summer. Brilliant red rose hips follow bloom, and the foliage turns bright orange in the fall. A very hardy species, it is especially good for seashore plantings because it can tolerate drought, poor soil, and salt spray, and can even be found on dunes facing the ocean. The species has a pink and a white form. Also worth considering are its descendants, the Hybrid Rugosa Shrub roses ('Frau Dagmar Hartopp' is much admired).

R. virginiana, a native to northeastern America, is 4–6' tall, a fast grower, salt tolerant, and a purplish fall color; has single fragrant pink flowers in June; and grows in sandy soils.

Another Wild Shrub rose to consider is *R. wichuraiana* (memorial rose), which bears small, white blossoms in late summer on glossy green, semi-evergreen foliage. The plants form mats that lie flat on the ground. Because it tolerates heat, drought, poor soil, and salt spray, it's an excellent groundcover for dune areas.

Finally, *R. nitida*, a wild native, to 2', with small rose-colored blossoms and small hips after bloom, is a charming plant that is more manageable for the small garden than the rugosas. The lustrous deep-green foliage turns brilliant red in the fall. This is one of the few roses that will tolerate poor drainage.

Climbing and Rambling Roses

The world of Climbing roses is large and includes Modern roses, Old Garden roses, and Wild roses. If you have the space, include climbers in your planting scheme, as they offer extravagant bloom. The

Rugosa roses on the water. The retaining wall helps control erosion.

plants do not attach themselves to surfaces, but must be tied to trellises, fences, and other supports. Many grow to 10–20'. The very pale pink 'New Dawn' is a popular large-flowered climber that is very hardy and can also be grown as a large shrub. A wild rambler that is both famously hardy and profuse in its bloom is the pale-yellow *R. banksiae lutea* (Lady Banks's rose), spring flowering and fragrant. It needs full sun. Ramblers have long, wandlike shoots that bear clusters of small flowers, and are ideal for filling open spaces or growing over a pergola or other structure. Two old reliable white ramblers are 'Sander's White' and 'Seagull.'

Miniature Roses

These are lilliputian versions of the larger varieties, growing to a mere 12" and sporting tiny blossoms. If space is a problem, and you want to grow roses, these are the best option.

Vines

Perennial vines are hardy to Zone 5, with many hardy to Zones 3 and 4. Annual vines will be killed by early frosts. Note that maximum growth height given is for optimal conditions. Many vines will be substantially less vigorous in seaside conditions.

***Ampelopsis brevipedunculata* (porcelain vine)**
Perennial. Grown primarily for its appealing fruit, clusters of pea-shaped berries that turn from pale lilac to yellow and finally to blue in the fall. Bright-green, textured foliage. Thrives in ordinary soil, in full sun or partial shade. Some drought tolerance, but water during dry spells. Plant outdoors in mid-spring or early fall. A vigorous grower suitable for secondary dune areas, and to cover fence or trellis rather quickly. *A. brevipedunculata* 'Elegant' has variegated leaves.

❦ *Campsis radicans* (trumpet vine)
Perennial. Scarlet, orange, or yellow trumpetlike blossoms on vigorous vines with medium-green foliage. Grows to 50'. Thrives in ordinary soil in full sun or partial shade. Drought resistant. Plant outdoors in midspring or fall. Do not plant on or near the facade of a house or outbuilding, as vines grow through any openings. I have one of these amazingly aggressive plants in the wrong place on my property and have tried to kill it for years, but every year it sports new shoots and grows. Its hardiness is an asset near the sea, and it is ideal for secondary dune areas. Cultivars: 'Crimson Trumpet,' dark-red flowers; 'Flamenco,' red flowers; 'Flava,' yellow flowers; 'Yellow Trumpet,' bright-yellow flowers.

❦ *Celastrus scandens* (American bittersweet)
Perennial. Grown for the orange and red berries that appear on the vines in fall, a good winter food source for birds. Thrives in ordinary soil in full sun or partial shade. Drought resistant. Plant outdoors anytime during the season. Need both male and female for fruit. The vines will choke any plant they climb on, including shrubs and trees, so be sure to keep them well pruned or plant them where they cannot attach to other plantings. Good selection for secondary dune areas.

Morning glory 'Heavenly Blue'—an all-time favorite. Below right: Fall-blooming clematis 'Bill MacKenzie'

Clematis

Perennial. White, pink, red, blue, yellow, lavender, purple, and combinations thereof. Saucerlike blossoms 1–9" in diameter, depending on variety, on vines sporting handsome medium-green, glossy foliage. The flowers are followed by silvery seed pods. Thrives in moderately fertile, slightly alkaline soil, in full sun or partial shade (the base of the plant should be shaded to keep roots cool). Requires moisture during summer drought. Plant in early to late spring. When planting, dig a hole 2' across and 2' deep and fortify the soil with substantial amounts of peat moss or compost so that moisture will be retained around the roots of the plant. This is essential to vigorous, healthy growth. Virtually carefree once established.

Pruning clematis is a complicated business, since some varieties should be cut back to about 1' in late winter, and others should merely be pruned to remove dead vines or to shape or contain the plant. It is best to check at point of purchase about pruning the particular variety that you have selected. The same holds true for the variety's growth habit, which may vary from 3' to 30'. By the way, if you prune your clematis the wrong way, you won't kill it; at worst, you may deprive yourself of blooms for that season.

C. paniculata (Sweet autumn clematis) Perennial. Masses of fragrant, small white blossoms in late summer on vigorous, 20–30' tangled vines with attractive, medium-green foliage. Thrives in ordinary soil, in full sun or partial shade. Drought resistant once established. Plant outdoors in midspring. Vigorous, yet easily controlled.

C. 'Romantika,' introduced in 2003 from eastern Europe, has reddish-purple flowers, is compact, and blooms from summer to fall.

Hydrangea anomala subsp. petiolaris (climbing hydrangea)

Perennial. Large, flat, 6–8" white or ivory blossom clusters and attractive deep-green foliage. To 75'. Deciduous, thrives in enriched soil in partial shade, so plant on the north side of the house. Start with a large specimen, at least a five-gallon pot, since it is slow to establish. Requires moisture, but is drought resistant once established. Plant outdoors in midspring. Usually sold as *H. petiolaris*. Can be trained to grow up the trunks of tall trees or buildings.

Variegated porcelain vine and climbing hydrangea

Ipomoea (morning glory)

Annual. Blossoms of sky blue, purple, pink, rose, red, white, or combinations thereof, on vigorous vines with large, heart-shaped, deep-green foliage. Thrives in ordinary soil, in full sun. Requires moisture, attracts hummingbirds and butterflies. Plant outdoors, in situ, after all danger of frost, according to package directions. Soak seeds overnight in lukewarm water to hasten germination. The all-time favorite is the lovely *I. tricolor* 'Heavenly Blue,' which dresses up any garden from midsummer to killing frost.

Ipomoea quamoclit (cypress vine)

Lacy leaf with 1½"-long scarlet tubular flowers that flare out at the mouth, forming a five-pointed star. Grows to 20'.

Lathyrus japonicus/L. latifolius (beach pea, perennial pea)

Perennial. Low sprawling plant, purple to rose-colored pealike blossoms on short vines with medium-green foliage. Thrives in ordinary soil, in full sun or partial shade. Plant outdoors in midspring or fall. A vigorous plant suited for dune plantings. Annual

L. odoratus (sweet pea) is also popular in seaside gardens. Blooms from spring to late summer.

❧ *Lonicera* (honeysuckle)
Perennial. A very large genus of plants with many varieties available. All sport delicate, fragrant, spiderlike pink, red, yellow, or white blossoms on vigorous, compact vines with medium-green foliage. Most offer berry displays in the fall. Most thrive in ordinary soil, in full sun. Drought resistant and recommended for the worst seashore conditions. Plant outdoors, from early spring to fall. For secondary dune areas, where vigorous, invasive growth is desired, select *L. tatarica.* Do not use this plant in sheltered seaside areas as it will take over the entire garden in no time flat. Some cultivars to try are: *L.* 'Alabama Crimson,' 10–20'; *L.* 'Blanche Sandman', 10–20'; and *L.* 'Belgica', 20–40'.

❧ *Parthenocissus tricuspidata* (Boston ivy)
Perennial. Ivy-shaped leaves of deep lustrous green that turn brilliant red in the fall. To 35'. The insignificant blue berries that appear in the fall are relished by birds. Thrives in ordinary soil in full sun or partial shade. Drought resistant. Plant outdoors in midspring or fall. An excellent plant for stone walls or facades, but will cover wooden stockade fences as well. *P. tricuspidata* 'Fenway Park,' with yellow-green foliage, is an interesting one, worth trying.

Phaseolus coccineus (scarlet runner bean)
Annual. Vigorous vine with brilliant scarlet, pealike blossoms on 15' vines followed by edible pods, medium-green foliage. Thrives in ordinary soil, in full sun or partial shade. Requires moisture. Plant outdoors, in situ, after all danger of frost. Rapid and strong summer growth. Train on trellises, posts, or fences; vine needs some support.

❧ *Polygonum aubertii* (silverlace)
Perennial. Panicles of white flowers in late summer, on medium-green foliage. To 20'. Thrives in sandy soil, in full sun. Drought resistant. Twining vine grows rapidly but will not harm shingles or wood walls. Needs severe pruning each spring, blooms in late summer.

Roses, climbing, see Roses (page 166)

❧ *Smilax glauca* (catbrier)
Perennial. Semi-evergreen native plant with medium-green leaves bearing blue-black berries in the fall. Vines occasionally have thorns. Thrives in ordinary soil in all light conditions. Drought resistant. Plant anytime from early spring to late fall. Suitable for secondary dune plantings. Too rampant for sheltered gardens.

Tropaeolum (nasturtium)
Annual. Yellow, orange, gold, and red funnel-shaped blossoms on 6–8' vines bearing pretty pea-green leaves. Thrives in ordinary soil in full sun. If soil is too rich, foliage will be lush but flowers will be few. Do not use high-nitrogen fertilizer, but feed plants high phosphorous fertilizer instead. Requires moisture during drought. Plant seeds outdoors after all danger of frost, according to package directions. Deadhead for continuous bloom. The pungent foliage is edible and can be used in salads. Recommended for the worst seashore conditions. Cultivars to try: *T. majus* 'Alaska'; *T. majus* 'Hermine Grashoff,' double; *T. majus* 'Variegatus,' variegated leaves, orange-red.

❧ *Vitis labrusca* (fox grape)
Perennial. An ancestor of American cultivated grapes, with grapelike leaves and small purple, amber, or brown-red grapes in fall. Wild fox grape thrives in ordinary soil, in full sun or partial shade, and grows to 30'. Drought resistant. Plant in spring or fall. Attracts Japanese beetles, so avoid this plant if you grow roses in your garden. Suitable for secondary dune areas. Too rangy for sheltered gardens.

❧ *Wisteria floribunda/Wisteria sinensis* (Japanese/Chinese wisteria)
Perennial. White, purple, lavender, or pink, highly fragrant, blossom clusters, 9–20" long on vigorous vines, with medium-green loosely structured foliage. To 50'. Thrives in ordinary soil, in full sun. Drought resistant once established. Plant in early spring. Avoid fertilizing plant as this will diminish bloom substantially. Wisteria often needs heavy pruning, particularly if planted on a trellis or pergola adjoining a house or near trees. It has been known to destroy a house if allowed to grow unchecked, but its vigor is an asset by the sea. An old-time favorite is *W. floribunda carnea,* the hardiest of all wisteria, with fragrant pale-pink flowers that will bloom for four weeks.

Shrubs & Trees

When you start a garden the first question to ask yourself is how much you need to change in the way of major plantings. Find out what you already have. Ask a knowledgeable person for help or buy a field guide that covers your area. Unless you have a really clear idea of what you want to do, leave the existing trees and shrubs alone for a season and see what they're like.

Often, there's a reason why they're there in the first place. If you were wondering why Ken Ruzicka (see page 81) would design a garden around such native trees as pitch pine, sour gum, American holly, and sassafras, ask yourself (as he surely did) what other trees would have a chance of becoming established on a low-lying, boggy stretch of barrier island. Remember also that many trees grow no faster than you do. If, like Katie Dennis (see page 19), you have a hillside of handsome shade trees and conifers rolling down to the water, consider that it would be a generation before anyone in your family has such magnificent shade again, should you cut them down.

Ed Rezek's secret dwarf conifer garden on Long Island.
Who says you need flowers to have color?

I'm not saying that you should never fell a tree or yank out a shrub and plant a new one. Just think about it first. There can serve many purposes. They can be used as single specimens to provide focal points in the garden, in foundation plantings, as windbreaks, as plantings to control erosion, to provide shade, in shrub borders or hedges along the edges of your property for privacy, and in borders to divide one area of your property from another.

You can buy shrubs and trees at a nursery or garden center, or from a mail-order company. If you buy by mail, it's best to get your orders in by January or February, but you can continue to place orders through the end of May. Will trees and shrubs be healthier or "fresher" if you buy them at a nursery? Not necessarily: most nurseries and garden centers purchase their stock from wholesale dealers, so buying it locally does not necessarily mean that it was grown locally. A tree or shrub purchased "on the ground," so to speak, however, is likely to be bigger, which may make a difference if you're in a hurry to see your garden as you envision it. Just don't expect the breadth of selection locally that you see in catalogues. Finally, a local gardening service with a good reputation can be a good source for purchasing and planting trees. A good service will take responsibility for the long-term health of the tree, and replace it if something goes wrong.

Trees and shrubs are usually sold in containers or bagged and burlapped (called B & B in the garden business). The burlap is usually very loosely woven and will eventually rot, so it is not necessary to remove it before installing a plant. Container-grown plants stand a better chance of surviving particularly harsh seaside environments than B & B stock. Avoid bare-root stock, and be careful of B & B stock late in the season, for if the nursery hasn't been conscientious about watering, what you take home may resemble a cannonball with a stick in it rather than a tree.

All shrubs included in this list are hardy to Zone 5, with many hardy to Zones 2 and 3. When buying shrubs and trees, make sure that the root ball is not dried out and that it is in proportion to the size of the plant. If a plant appears too large for its container, it may be pot bound; pot-bound trees or shrubs often develop roots that circle around and eventually choke the plant. Choose larger specimens so that you can get a head start on your landscaping.

Prunus maritima *(beach plum), a familiar sight near Atlantic beaches.*

Variegated weigela blooms from spring to fall. Its bell-shaped flowers attract hummingbirds.

Shrubs

Aronia arbutifolia 'Brilliantissima' (chokeberry)
Deciduous cultivar of the native shrub. White five-petaled blossoms in spring are followed by vivid red berries, on medium-green foliage which turns bright red in autumn. 3–8", but can be controlled by pruning. Prefers moist conditions, but will thrive in seaside gardens and will naturalize. If possible, water regularly during summer drought.

Aronia melanocarpa (black chokeberry)
Deciduous native shrub. White blossoms in spring and black berries in fall on medium-green foliage. 2–6'. 'Autumn Magic' can grow to 6' high and 6' wide.

✿ Baccharis halimifolia (groundsel, sea myrtle)
Deciduous native shrub or small tree. Separate male and female plants. Female plants produce paint-brush-shaped fruits with white, thistlelike blossoms in late summer on coarse, yellow-green foliage. 4–15', but can be controlled by pruning. Groundsel is highly tolerant of salt spray and can be planted in the spring or early fall very near the shoreline in sandy soil. Drought resistant.

✿ Berberis thunbergii (Japanese barberry)
A large group of deciduous shrubs that have a wide variety of attributes. Red berries in fall and foliage of red, yellow, purple, dark green, or with variegations, depending on variety. 2–5'. Thrives in sandy soil. Drought resistant. A compact, thorny shrub often used for hedges because it takes pruning well. The thorns tend to collect debris, which can be difficult to remove. Seeds itself; can be invasive. Varieties: *B. thunbergii* 'Atropurpurea Nana,' dwarf, 2', red/purple foliage; *B. thunbergii* 'Helmond Pillar,' upright, 5', red-purple foliage.

✿ Buddleia davidii (butterfly bush, summer lilac)
Deciduous shrub. Showy lilaclike spikes of white, yellow, deep blue, pink, red, or purple clusters of blossoms on medium-green foliage. 6–15', but can be controlled by pruning. Drought resistant. Foliage dies down to the ground in the winter, growing again to mature height in spring. Cut back to 4–6" in late fall or early spring before new growth commences. 'African Queen' has dark purple flowers; 'Opera' has pink flowers in clusters to 2'; 'Dartmoor,' a new variety, has many lavender spikes instead of only one spike at the end of each branch.

Buxus microphylla (boxwood)
The traditional evergreen shrub for hedges, tightly branched, with small lustrous leaves. 3–30', depending on variety, of which there are many in cultivation. Thrives in sun or partial shade and in ordinary soil. Drought tolerant once established. Not hardy north of Zone 6 and not used more widely because of its susceptibility to extreme cold. Dwarf forms are ideal for edging beds. *B. sempervirens* can grow to 30'.

Caryopteris × clandonensis (bluebeard)
Deciduous shrub. Spikes of blue or purplish blue blossoms in late summer and fall on silvery green foliage. 3–4'. Cut back to 6" in late winter or early spring. If location is ideal, plant will self-sow. You can avoid seedlings by cutting all flowering stems after bloom, but you may find the plant so attractive and useful that you will want lots of them to transplant elsewhere in the garden. Hardy to Zone 5. 'First Choice,' compact, deep blue, requires little pruning; 'Dark Knight,' compact, intense blue, 3–4', blooms midsummer.

Ceanothus ovatus (wild lilac)

Deciduous native shrub. Small clusters of white blossoms on medium-green foliage. To 3'. This and *C. americanus*, which is too rangy in habit for garden use in my opinion, is the only variety of *Ceanothus* appropriate for temperate regions. The popular *C.* × *delilianus* grows only in subtropical climates.

Chamaecyparis (false cypress)

Coniferous shrub. Globular, pyramidal, and spreading forms in silver, blue, green, or gold foliage, depending on variety. Recommended dwarf varieties include:

C. obtusa 'Aurea Nana' (dwarf gold Hinoki cypress): heavy gold foliage.

C. obtusa 'Kosteri Nana': lacy foliage, broad growth habit.

C. obtusa 'Tortulosa Nana' (dwarf twisted branch cypress): branches are twisted, compact irregular pyramidal form.

C. obtusa 'Gracilis Nana': deep-green foliage, upright growth habit.

Hibiscus 'Diane' (rose-of-Sharon). Unlike common rose-of-Sharon, this sterile type does not sport seedlings everywhere.

C. pisifera 'Argentea Nana' (dwarf silver cypress): soft, plumed silvery blue foliage; dense globular growth habit. 'Argentea Variegata Nana' has variegated foliage.

C. pisifera 'Aurea Pendula' (dwarf gold thread cypress): bright golden pendulous filaments; dense low-growing shrub. Does not burn in sun.

C. pisifera 'Minima' (dwarf threadleaf cypress): green foliage; compact growth habit.

C. pisifera 'Sulphuria Nana' (dwarf sulfur cypress): bright sulfur-colored foliage; broad growth habit.

C. pisifera filifera 'Aurea Variegata Nana' (dwarf gold variegated cypress): gold variegated foliage.

Chamaecyparis nootkatensis 'Pendula' (weeping Alaska cedar)

Evergreen, slow growing, 30–45', drought tolerant when established. Dramatic specimen tree with drooping branches and needlelike leaves.

❧ Clethra alnifolia (sweet pepperbush, summersweet)

Deciduous native shrub. Spikes of white or pink flowers in late summer followed by black seeds that look like peppercorns, on medium-green foliage. 4–6'. Thrives in wet or dry sandy soil and in sun or partial shade. Tolerant of salt spray.

Comptonia peregrina (sweet fern)

Deciduous native shrub, 2–4', fernlike shrub with aromatic leaves. Requires moisture in sandy acidic soil, full sun to partial shade, adapts to wetland conditions, but difficult to transplant. A refreshing tea can be made from the leaves.

Cornus sericea (red osier dogwood)

Deciduous native shrub. Small white blossoms in late spring and white berries in summer, on medium-green foliage. Full sun to patial shade, to 12'. The red bark is particularly lovely in the snow. *C. sericea* 'Flaviramea' (golden-twig dogwood) sports yellow stems.

❧ Cotoneaster

Broad-leaved evergreen shrub. A wide range of cultivars either upright or creeping, most with white or pink blossoms in spring and red berries in fall, on lustrous, deep-green foliage. 2–20', depending on variety. Drought resistant once established. Cotoneaster is especially useful to cover a sunny bank or to control erosion. Tough and fast-growing varieties particularly suited to the seaside garden include:

C. *dammeri* (bearberry cotoneaster): low-growing (18") and useful as a groundcover, although technically a shrub.

C. *divaricatus* (spreading cotoneaster): a carefree shrub that sports brilliant yellow-and-red longlasting foliage in the fall, to 6'.

C. *horizontalis* (rock cotoneaster): another lower-growing variety (24–36") that makes a beautiful fall display.

❧ Cytisus scoparius (Scotch broom)
Deciduous or semi-evergreen shrub. Yellow, crimson, apricot, lilac, and tricolor, pealike blossoms on upright shrub with needlelike foliage. To 6'. Thrives in full sun and in sandy soil. Drought resistant. Tolerant of salt spray. The common yellow is very invasive weed and is destructive to natural areas. I recommend 'Lilac Time,' a noninvasive variety.

Forsythia
Deciduous shrub. Yellow or cream-colored blossoms in early spring, on upright or weeping shrub with bright green foliage. 1–8'. Avoid weeping versions as they require annual pruning to keep them under control once established. Upright varieties such as *F.* × *intermedia* 'Lynwood Gold' are recommended. Prune after flowering rather than in fall or early spring for most profuse display each season. Try *F. koreana kumson*, with silver-edged leaves that look spectacular after it blooms, 4', drought tolerant. A rare but available white forsythia, *Abeliophyllum distichum,* is a must, with creamy white flowers and golden stamens, 5'.

❧ Gaylussacia baccata (black huckleberry)
Deciduous native shrub. Reddish flowers followed by dark-blue edible berries. Small green leaves turn red in fall. To 36". Thrives in wet or dry sandy soil. Drought resistant. Common in coastal heathlands of Long Island.

❧ Genista (broom)
Deciduous or semi-evergreen shrub. A group of useful plants for the seaside environment, similar to *Cytisus*. Select from the following: G. *tinctoria* (dyer's greenweed), now naturalized in the eastern part of the United States, with yellow pealike blossoms in early June that can be used to make yellow dye, to 36"; G.

The graceful, cold-tolerant Chamaecyparis nootkatensis 'Pendula' (weeping Alaska cedar) is native to the Pacific Northwest.

sagittalis (arrow broom), an excellent groundcover (to 20") in sandy soil and hot sun, with yellow pealike flowers in late spring. Drought resistant.

Hebe
Broad-leaved evergreen shrub. White or pink blossoms on leathery foliage. Like pachysandra, *Hebe* can be easily propagated from cuttings. Two varieties are appropriate for seaside gardens: *H.* × *andersonii*, a white, late-summer blooming species, to 4'; 'Variegata,' with leaves edged in cream, is widely available; *H. decumbens* (ground hebe), with small gray leaves edged in red and small spikes of white blossoms in spring; *H.* 'Franciscana Blue Gem,' 40", rich violet-blue dense flowers.

❧ Hibiscus syriacus (rose-of-Sharon, althaea)
Deciduous shrub or small tree. An old-fashioned favorite, cultivated in North America for over two hundred years. White, white-and-burgundy, or rose blossoms, resembling the southern hibiscus, on medium-green foliage. To 15'. Recent hybrids, such as 'Diane,' are a stunning white and do not reseed all over the place. Nearly indestructible.

Not only is Hollywood juniper (Juniperus chinensis) salt and wind tolerant, but it is very sculptural looking as well.

Hippophae rhamnoides (sea buckthorn)
Deciduous shrub. Willowlike gray-green foliage with silvery underside. Small, yellowish blossoms are inconspicuous, but fall berries are bright orange and profuse. To 30'. Thrives in full sun and sandy soil. Drought resistant. Both male and female plants are necessary for fruiting. As the berries are very acidic, birds are not attracted to them and they persist throughout the fall and into winter. 'Leikora,' female, heavy fruiting form; 'Sprite,' compact, 2', great for low seaside hedges.

Hydrangea macrophylla (French hydrangea)
Deciduous shrub. The classic summer seashore plant. Large blue, white, or pink pompon-shaped blossoms in mid- to late summer, on handsome deep-green foliage. 3–6'. Tolerates shade. Roots prefer moist conditions, so be sure to provide sufficient water during summer drought. Plant will tell you if it needs watering by wilting visibly. If you want blue bloom, try scratching one tablespoon of an acid fertilizer such as Miracid into the ground around the plant when shoots first emerge in spring. For pink bloom, substitute one tablespoon of garden lime.

Juniperus (juniper)
Coniferous shrub. Creeping, low and spreading, vase-shaped and columnar, with varying shades of green, blue, or gold foliage. The toughest of the junipers is *J. conferta* (shore juniper), a low, spreading shrub (1–2' high to 8' in width) that will often grow directly on ocean dunes. It is particularly useful in binding the soil with its roots. Other recommended varieties include:

J. chinensis 'Japonica' (Japanese juniper): semi-upright in habit; deeply textured foliage in slate to green shades.

J. chinensis 'Blue Vase' (blue vase juniper): vase-shaped growth habit, to 5'.

J. chinensis 'Old Gold' (old gold juniper): golden yellow.

J. chinensis 'Pfitzerana Aurea' (gold tip juniper): bright golden in spring and summer.

J. chinensis 'Torulosa' (Hollywood juniper): dense shrub with twisted branches, to 6'. Recommended for the worst seashore conditions.

J. chinensis var. *procumbens* 'Nana' (dwarf Japanese juniper, pronina juniper): short, stiff branches forming a carpet up to 6' across, mounding to 10" in the center.

J. horizontalis 'Bar Harbor' (Bar Harbor juniper): creeping form; steel-blue foliage with a fernlike appearance.

J. horizontalis 'Blue Chip' (blue chip juniper): silvery blue foliage; spreading, low mounding habit.

J. horizontalis 'Glauca' (blue creeping juniper): creeping form, blue foliage.

J. horizontalis 'Plumosa' (Andorra juniper): low spreading habit, summer foliage is silvery green, turning purple after frost.

J. rigida 'Pendula' (weeping needle juniper): narrow, tall, and pendant in habit.

Kolkwitzia amabilis (beautybush)
Deciduous shrub. My own feeling is that beautybush is overused in North America, but this 10', full sun, medium-green foliaged shrub thrives in dry sandy soil and can be used as a windbreak and transplants easily. Drought resistant. Most specimens sport washed-out pink blossoms, but look for deeper pink blooming plants at local nurseries; they are often called 'Rosea.' Seed clusters follow the blossoms and the brown bark falls from stems in long strips. Autumn foliage is red.

Ligustrum (privet)
Deciduous or semi-evergreen shrub. Privet bears white flower clusters in the spring, but is of course grown primarily for its glossy foliage. To 15'. This ubiquitous hedging plant is used for windbreaks and privacy screening. Drought resistant. High pruning the trunk results in an interesting treelike form. There are numerous varieties to choose from, especially *L. ovalifolium* (California privet) and *L. vulgare* (common privet).

Myrica pensylvanica (bayberry)
Semi-evergreen native shrub. Silvery-gray berries in autumn on glossy, aromatic foliage. To 9', although usually 4–5', full sun to partial shade. Berries are used to make bayberry oil and bayberry candles. Thrives in sand and withstands salt spray. Drought resistant. Can be grown very close to the ocean. Recommended for the worst seashore conditions.

Pieris japonica (andromeda)
Broad-leaved evergreen shrub. Small clusters of white blossoms in spring on lustrous 3½"-long leaves. 6'. Andromeda is one of the earliest of the

broad-leafed evergreens to bloom and therefore useful in combination with early spring-blooming bulbs such as daffodils and hyacinths. Deer resistant. Thrives in partial shade and moist soil. 'Bisbee Dwarf,' 'Bonsai,' and 'Pygmaea' are dwarf forms. 'Cavatine' is cold hardy, compact, and later blooming.

Pinus, see Trees (page 181)

Potentilla fruticosa (bush cinquefoil)

Deciduous native shrub. Small yellow or white blossoms throughout summer and into fall on foliage that resembles strawberry leaves. To 4'. Will not bloom unless grown in full sun. Survives in poor, dry soil with little moisture, but will of course grow better in enriched soil and with regular watering. There are many named varieties available: 'Beesii,' 'Katherine Dykes,' and 'Vilmoriniana' sport silver foliage. New varieties come in new colors: 'Daydawn,' with creamy pink flowers is very attractive; 'Red Ace' has eye-catching red flowers.

❦ Prunus maritima (beach plum)

Deciduous native shrub. A dense, compact shrub, to 6'. White flowers in the spring become small blue or red plums that can be made into delicious jelly or jam. Leaves turn red in the fall. Thrives in full sun. Tolerates sandy soil, shade, wind, and salt spray. Drought resistant. Hybridizers have been busy creating varieties that produce larger fruits with red color, such as 'Eastham,' 'Hancock,' and 'Premier.' Recommended for the worst seashore conditions.

Prunus pumila (sand cherry)

Deciduous shrub. White flowers and purple-black fruit on purple foliage. To 8', but can be contained by pruning. Tolerates sandy soil.

Rosa, see Roses (page 166)

Spiraea (bridal wreath)

Deciduous shrub. Graceful arching branches completely covered with white, pink, or red blossoms in late spring, on medium-green foliage. To 6', depending on variety. Needs sun and is not drought tolerant. Prune in fall every few years to maintain vigor: remove branches at soil level, not by cutting them halfway down. Fountain-shaped *S. × vanhouttei* is the most commonly planted variety.

Symphoricarpos orbiculatus (coralberry)

Deciduous shrub. A densely branched plant grown for its colorful purple-red berries in late summer and fall. The spring yellow blossoms are inconspicuous. 7'. Roots help retain bank or dune soil. *S. orbiculatus* 'Leucocarpus' sports white berries; 'Hancock,' 2', is used as a groundcover.

Syringa (lilac)

Deciduous shrub or small tree. Pink, white, lilac, blue, or deep-purple clusters of florets in late spring on medium-green foliage. Thrives in full sun. *S. vulgaris* (common lilac) is too tall for borders (it grows to 20'), but can be used for screens or planted in a grove in the distance. Lilacs that grow to a more manageable height and thrive in a seaside environment include *S. × persica* (Persian lilac), with deep-purple blooms (6') and *S. oblata dilatata* (Korean early lilac), with pink blooms (5–6'). Deadhead flowers for more profuse bloom following year.

❦ Tamarix (tamarisk, salt cedar)

Deciduous shrub or small tree. Fluffy pink blossoms in the spring on feathery foliage. To 15'. Prune after bloom. Tolerates poor soil, wind, and salt spray. Drought resistant. Recommended for the worst seashore conditions.

❦ Taxus (yew)

Coniferous shrub. Medium to deep green needles on columnar, moundlike, and globular plants. Drought resistant. The following varieties are particularly useful in the seaside garden: *T. cuspidata* 'Densiformis' (spreading Japanese yew), a mound-shaped shrub, spreading to 6', with medium-green needles, that can be sheared to make hedges; *T. fairview* (Fairview yew), globular and compact in growth habit; and *T.* 'Aurea Nana' (golden dwarf yew), a dwarf with bright yellow-green foliage.

Thuja occidentalis (American arborvitae)

Coniferous native shrub. Pyramidal, conical, globular, and columnar forms with gold and light- to dark-green foliage. Grows to 60', but can be dwarfed by vigorous pruning. Tolerates salt spray and sandy soil. Two valuable varieties are 'Hetz's Midget' (dwarf globe arborvitae), a slow-growing, globular shrub with medium-green foliage and 'Woodwardii' (Woodward globe arborvitae), a bushy shrub that can even be used in window boxes. Tall versions are excellent for a privacy hedge.

❧ Vaccinium corymbosum (highbush blueberry)
Deciduous native shrub. A tried-and-true classic for the seaside garden. Inconspicuous white flowers followed by blueberries that ripen in early summer on handsome deep-green foliage that turns brilliant red in the fall, a source of food for many birds, 6–12'. Drought resistant and adapts to wetland conditions.

❧ Viburnum
Deciduous shrub. Viburnums prefer sun and tolerate salt spray. Recommended varieties include:

V. carlesii: waxy fragrant blossoms, tinged pink in early spring, on gray-green foliage that turns bronze-red in fall, to 6"; shapely growth habit.

V. dentatum (arrowwood): a native that adapts to wetland conditions, with attractive clusters of white blossoms in spring, followed by blue berries, on deep green foliage that turns bright red in autumn, 8–14'.

V. opulus (European cranberry) or *V. trilobum* (American cranberry): Large, flat clusters of white blossoms in spring followed by bright-red fruit, on handsome deep-green foliage that turns bright crimson in fall, to 12'. Select varieties of either listed as 'Compactum,' 6', or 'Nanum,' 2–3', if space is at a premium. These species are almost identical, but some horticulturists hold that *V. trilobum* has better autumn color, and it is a native that has adapted equally well to wetland and shoreline conditions. The fruit is edible but not to everyone's taste.

V. prunifolium (black haw): An old-fashioned favorite for seaside plantings, with flat, white clusters of spring blossoms and blue-black fruit in late summer and fall, on dark green foliage that turns maroon then deep red in fall, growing to 15' but very accepting of pruning as either a shrub or small tree. Plants are dense enough to form hedges, with fruit that has been used in preserves since the Colonial era.

Weigela
Deciduous shrub. Pink, white, red, peach, and lavender trumpet-shaped blossoms, depending on cultivar. Bloom in late spring–early summer. Prefers partial shade where summers are hot. Weigela requires little care, but after a few years, should be pruned at soil level after the shrub blooms. *W.* 'Java Red,' 4', is not as rangy as the taller ones. *W. florida* 'Variegata,' with its variegated leaves, is very popular, flowers May–June. New small hybrids are now available. *W. florida* 'Elvera,' dark burgundy foliage, pink flowers, low mounding, grows to only 3'.

Trees

Trees on this list have been divided between evergreens (particularly conifers) and deciduous trees, which lose their leaves in the fall. Generally speaking, the mature height of trees depends entirely on growing conditions. Specimens grown near the ocean rarely reach their full height and are subject to a phenomenon called wind pruning.

EVERGREEN TREES

Abies concolor (white Colorado fir)
Pyramid form. Blue-green, 2" needles, 40–80'. Prefers full sun and ordinary soil and is drought resistant once established. Perhaps the most heat resistant of all evergreens. Among the best selections are 'Violacea,' with bluish-white needles, and 'Conica,' a slow-growing dwarf variety.

❧ Cedrus atlantica 'Glauca' (blue Atlas cedar)
Pyramid form. Tight whorls of short, silver-green needles, 60–120'. Attractive cones persist through winter. Prefers full sun and ordinary soil. Drought resistant once established. Atlas cedar, one of the most handsome evergreens for seaside plantings, will cast a deep shade.

❧ Cedrus deodara (deodar cedar)
Pyramid form. Elegant tree with weeping branches and somewhat longer needles than Atlas cedar. In landscape to 80' but in the wild to 150'. 'Pendula' has branches that often touch the ground; 'Glauca' has blue-green or silver-gray needles. Prefers full sun and ordinary soil. Drought resistant once established.

❧ Chamaecyparis (false cypress)
Conical or columnar forms. A very large group of evergreen trees with very small, scalelike leaves, in various shades of green, blue-green, and silver, many with variegated coloring of yellow, white, or silver. Useful as a hedge or a lawn decoration. Most thrive in full sun and tolerate drought conditions and sandy soil. Consult locally for recommended cultivars.

Cryptomeria japonica (Japanese cedar)
Conical form. Elegant evergreen with small, short needles. 3–150', depending on variety. Bark shreds, creating trunk interest 'Sakkan-sugi,' compact, 15–20', yellow-green foliage, fast grower. 'Yoshino,'

most available in northeastern nurseries, 30', fast grower, blue-green summer foliage bronzes in the winter.

Ilex (holly)

A large group of useful trees and shrubs suitable for seaside environments. Hollies generally need sun to fruit out successfully, as well as a well-drained light soil. They are dioecious, which means that there needs to be a male within about one-half mile of a female if you want fruiting trees. Both sexes bear flowers, but only the female bears berries. Recommended varieties include:

I. cornuta (Chinese holly): Large, dark, shiny green leaves and red fruit. Compact form. 'Dwarf Burford' can be sheared into a dense, formal hedge. Drought tolerant, but not reliable north of Zone 7. Female plants set fruit without a male plant.

I. crenata (Japanese holly): Fine, glossy leaves and small black fruit. Various forms, most adaptable to shearing for hedges. Needs protection in Zone 6.

I. glabra (inkberry): Inconspicuous black berries in late summer and fall on deep-green shiny oval leaves. Male and female plants are necessary for fruiting. Tolerates salt spray but not very dry soil. Responds well to pruning.

I. opaca (American holly): The hardiest holly. Dark green leaves and small red or orange fruit. Conical or open form, to 50', but much shorter on the shore. Native to seashore environments Long Island and south. Can be used for tall hedges. Tolerates shade. Many varieties available.

I. pedunculosa (longstalk holly): Glossy oval leaves and red fruit on 1½" stalks. Similar in habit to American holly.

I. verticillata (winterberry): Native deciduous shrub with many available garden varieties sporting different leaves and berries ranging from red to orange to yellow, 4–15'. Plant red-fruiting cultivars to attract birds. Winterberry grows best in full sun in very wet soil, but drought-tolerant varieties are available.

I. × *altaclerensis* (highclere holly): Large glossy leaves, often spineless, and red fruit. Small tree or large shrub. Somewhat tolerant of salt spray, but not reliable north of Zone 7.

I. × *meserveae* (Blue holly): Spiny blue-green leaves and red fruit. Rounded, compact form, 5–8'. Can be used for low, informal hedges. Not reliable north of Zone 6.

Juniperus virginiana (eastern red cedar)

Native, tough, and planted everywhere. Conical or columnar form. Slow-growing tree with small, scale-like leaves and blue cones that resemble berries. 100', but rarely exceeds 30' near the shore. Transplants well. Thrives in full sun in ordinary to poor soil. Drought resistant once established. Can be used as a screen or hedge. Recommended for the worst seashore conditions. 'Emerald Sentinel,' new, 20', dark-green foliage, female variety.

Picea (spruce)

A large group of trees with short blue or green needles in mounded, conical, pendulous, and columnar forms. Thrives in full sun or partial shade and in ordinary soil. Drought resistant once established. Dwarf or slow-growing varieties suitable for seashore gardens include:

P. glauca var. *albertiana* (Alberta spruce): conical dwarf with medium-green needles.

P. mariana 'Nana' (dwarf black spruce): mound-shaped with short, light gray-green needles.

P. pungens 'Glauca' (dwarf blue spruce): conical dwarf with blue needles.

P. pungens 'Globosa' (dwarf globe blue spruce): globe-shaped tree with silvery blue needles.

Pinus (pine)

A large group of trees with long needles in shades of green and blue-green in mounded, columnar, pendulous, and conical shapes. Thrives in full sun or partial shade in ordinary soil and resists drought once established.

Recommended dwarf varieties include:

P. mugo (mugo pine): Low growing (and slow growing) moundlike pine with long, bright green needles, 5–20' depending on variety. Very hardy. 'Amber Gold', slow growing. Needles turn a delightful golden amber in the winter.

P. nigra (Australian pine, European pine): 40–60' tall, 20–40' wide. Needs full sun and tolerates a range of soil conditions. Tolerates salt spray well and is excellent as a windbreak, but can also be used as a specimen tree.

P. pumila (dwarf Siberian stone pine): Spreading habit with light blue-green to blue needles, 2–3'.

P. strobus 'Nana' (dwarf white pine): Bushy habit with feathery blue-green needles.

P. strobus 'Ontario' (dwarf Ontario white pine): Spreading habit with feathery blue-green needles.

Pinus thunbergiana (*Japanese black pine*) *grows within yards of the ocean, setting off a colorful annual garden of Persian shield* (Strobilanthes dyerianus) *and blue salvia at Hereford Inlet Lighthouse and gardens, Wildwood, New Jersey.*

P. sylvestris 'Watereri' (dwarf Scotch pine): Compact slow growing form of Scotch pine, conical when young becoming rounded with age.

Recommended taller varieties include:

P. rigida (pitch pine): A scrubby native with dark green needles that thrives in very difficult rocky or sandy soil, especially at the seashore. To 75'.

P. sylvestris (Scotch pine): Compact, bushy tree adapting well to seaside conditions. Very hardy.

P. thunbergiana (Japanese black pine): An irregular, conical pine with bright green needles that thrives in a seashore environment. However, be advised! Despite the fact that this tree is almost universally recommended for seaside use, especially for windbreaks, a disease is killing them everywhere. Seek the advice of a knowledgeable gardener or your local Cooperative Extension agent before planting.

DECIDUOUS TREES

Acer

Majestic shade trees that are useful in borders and near ponds. Their red buds provide color in the spring, as their brilliant leaves do in the fall. 5'–over 100'. Most maples are slow growers and are adaptable to various growing conditions. They all have surface roots that absorb most of the moisture from the surrounding soil. Underplant only with shade loving, drought resistant groundcovers or install pebbles or wood chips to retain moisture.

A. griseum (paperbark maple): Dark-green trifoliate leaves cast light shade and develop good fall color. Bark is an especially attractive cinnamon brown and strips from trunk naturally throughout growing season. Roundish shape to 25'. Prefers sun or partial shade and ordinary soil and is moderately drought resistant once established.

A. platanoides (Norway maple): An excellent shade tree, roundish in shape and densely branched, with dark-green, leathery leaves. Usually 40–60' but can reach 80'. Prefers sun or partial shade and ordinary soil and is drought resistant once established. Autumn foliage is brilliant yellow or orange-red. Its brittle branches tend to split and break during heavy windstorms, and some people feel it is too intensively used. Sends seeds everywhere and can become a pest. Consult locally for recommended cultivars.

A. *pseudoplatanus* (sycamore maple): Especially suited to a seaside environment. If you have space for one large tree, select this one. Five-lobed leaves in various colors, depending on variety. To 90'. Prefers sun or partial shade and ordinary soil and is drought resistant and salt tolerant once established. There is no colorful autumn foliage display. Variegated forms are: 'Liopoldii' with yellow, green, and purple coloring, and 'Brilliantissimum,' with pink leaves that progress to cream, yellow, and finally green. Consult locally for other recommended cultivars.

A. rubrum (red maple): This native maple is not the familiar Japanese maple. It derives its name from the fact that its spring blossoms are bright red. Dark-green leaves and excellent fall color. Fast growing, 40–70', it splits easily during windstorms. Prefers full sun or partial shade. Adapts to wetland conditions. 'Autumn Flame,' round habit, 60', wonderful fall color. Consult locally for other recommended cultivars.

Amelanchier canadensis (shadbush, shadblow, serviceberry, juneberry)

Small native tree sporting single white flowers in early spring, followed by silver-gray foliage that turns yellow and red in fall. 6–20', but can be controlled by pruning. Thrives in ordinary soil and tolerates shade. Colorful, reddish-purple fall berries are relished by the birds. The more vigorous

Wild maples that filled this part of the property were cleared except for the clump near the water. A peaceful niche was created using very little color, to maintain the tranquil effect.

A. arborea is similar, and has larger flowers. Adapts to wetland conditions.

Betula pendula (European white birch)

Pyramidal weeping tree with white bark and small, glossy dark-green leaves. To 60'. Prefers full sun and normal soil and is drought resistant once established. Its brittle branches make it susceptible to damage in heavy winds. Subject to bronze birch borer infestation and short-lived, but its white bark is irresistible. 'Youngii' and 'Tristis' are weeping forms. Consult locally for other recommended cultivars. The native white birch, B. populifolia, is a smaller tree that often has multiple trunks.

Betula nigra (river birch)

Deciduous tree with fast growth rate, grows to 40–75', tolerates cold winters, thrives in the heat of summer, full sun, loamy soil, has lovely cinnamon colored bark that peels during the fall and winter. Great as a specimen tree; allow lots of room to showcase it.

Catalpa speciosa (Northern catalpa)

Distinguished by its large, handsome leaves and clusters of white bell-shape blossoms in summer, which are followed by long pods. Fast grower to 60'. Prefers full sun and ordinary soil. Drought resistant. A popular tree for difficult areas because it is vigorous in hot, dry environments.

Celtis occidentalis (hackberry)

Native shade tree with glossy dark-green leaves and dark-purple fruits that attract birds. Good yellow fall color. 30–60'. Prefers full sun and ordinary soil and is drought resistant. A good choice for difficult areas because it tolerates hot, dry environments, but it is subject to a number of diseases, including leaf disfiguration. Has orangey-red fleshy fruit in early fall.

Cercis canadensis (redbud)

Early spring-flowering native, deciduous, offering a profusion of small, purple-pink blossoms that are followed by dried pods later. Heart-shaped leaves turn a brilliant yellow in the fall. 25'. Prefers full sun and ordinary soil and is drought resistant once established. *C. canadensis* 'Alba' and 'Royal White' sports white blossoms. 'Covey' (Lavender Twist) is a weeping form.

Crataegus (hawthorn)

This small tree bears either white or pinkish-red blossoms in spring and red fruit in summer. Leaves are a glossy dark green and autumn foliage is brilliant red. Prefers full sun and ordinary soil and is drought resistant once established. *C. crus-galli* (cockspur) and *C. phaenopyrum* (Washington hawthorn), both natives, are the two best cultivars for all environments, both growing to 25'. Because their branches are thick with razor-sharp thorns, hawthorns are not good to plant where children play. 'Princeton Sentry,' however, is almost thornless. An unarmed variety of cockspur is also available.

Elaeagnus angustifolia (Russian olive)

Spreading shrublike tree distinguished by its elegant, silvery foliage. Yellowish flowers in early spring are followed by silver berries in fall. 15'. Thrives in full sun and in sandy soil, and is tolerant of salt spray. Drought resistant. Grows fast and likes an occasional pruning. Birds are attracted by berries. *E. umbellata* (autumn olive) is similar. 'Red King,' a clone, offers abundant deep-red fruits.

Fraxinus (ash)

A fast growing native shade tree, with handsome compound foliage. 50–80'. Prefers full sun and ordinary soil and is drought resistant once established. This vigorous tree is an excellent selection for seaside gardens. Select either *F. americana* (white ash), spectacular in yellow and purple in the fall, or the tougher *F. pennsylvanica* (green ash), with darker leaves and a more modest fall display. 'Bergeson,' extremely hardy, fast growing to 50', has yellow fall color.

Gleditsia triacanthos (thornless common honeylocust)

Delicate bright-green foliage and fragrant pendulous clusters of white blossoms in late spring. 30–60'. Autumn foliage is yellow. Good drought and salt tolerance. If you like the tree but not the seedpods that litter the ground in late summer, select a seedless variety.

Lagerstroemia 'Natchez' (crape myrtle)

Grown for its cinnamon-colored, smooth bark and lovely white flowers, this elegant tree likes sun to partial shade. 20–30'. Zone 7–9. Blooms early summer to fall.

Malus (flowering crab apple)

Beautiful small tree, bearing white, pink, or deep-red blossoms in spring. Many varieties offer edible small, red crab apples in summer and fall. (Technically, crab apples are apples less than 2" in diameter.) To 25'. Prefers full sun and moist soil, but is drought resistant once established. Dwarf and semidwarf varieties are available for use on patios and for small gardens. Standard sized trees can be used as specimen trees, in borders, as backdrops. 'Louisa,' bright-pink single flowers, ½" yellow fruit, upright broad weeping, 15'. It is a good idea to check at a reliable local nursery for varieties recommended for your area.

Nyssa sylvatica (pepperidge, sour gum, black gum, beetlebung, black tupelo)

An East Coast native whose many common names testify to its wide appeal. Handsome leathery, dark-green leaves turn brilliant orange to scarlet in fall. 30–50'. Thrives in full sun or partial shade, and in ordinary to moist soil. Drought resistant and also adapts to wetland conditions. Purchase only small specimens, since taproot damage can kill tree. 'Miss Scarlet,' deep-green leaves in summer and brilliant red in the fall.

Platanus × acerifolia (London plane)
This hybrid of native and European cultivars is an excellent tree for difficult areas where there is a lot of space for it to spread. Large, coarse maplelike leaves and exceptional bark. 75–100'. Prefers full sun and ordinary soil, and is drought resistant once established. 'Yardwood' is a new introduction that tolerates adverse conditions and is resistant to disease.

Prunus cerasifera (flowering plum)
Small flowering tree with white flowers in early spring followed by edible plumlike fruit and glossy leaves. To 25'. Prefers full sun and ordinary soil, and is drought resistant once established. Look for varieties with purple leaves, like 'Nigra,' 'Rosea,' or 'Thundercloud.' 'Newport,' one of the hardiest, purple leaves, 15–20'.

Prunus serotina (black cherry)
A native tree sporting white flowers in spring followed by small red fruits that turn black when mature. Elegant, lustrous foliage. To 60'. Easily grown, prefers full sun, ordinary soil and is drought resistant once established. Birds love the fruit, which can be used for sauces and desserts. 'White Sparkle' blooms profusely, and great fall display.

Quercus alba (white oak)
The sturdy, familiar native tree. Dark-green lobed leaves turn purplish-red in autumn. To 80'. Slow growing. Prefers full sun and ordinary soil. Drought resistant once established.

Quercus palustris (pin oak)
Dense, native of swampy woodlands. Graceful, drooping branches with glossy jagged leaves that turn brilliant red in fall. To 75'. Thrives in full sun and ordinary soil. Drought resistant once established. Note that oaks are usually substantially dwarfed when grown in a seaside environment. 'Crownright,' more upright form.

Robinia pseudoacacia (black locust)
Native with light-green oval leaves bearing pendulous clusters of fragrant white blossoms in late spring. To 75'. Prefers full sun and ordinary soil.

Drought resistant once established. Can be invasive. 'Frisia' is an unusual variety grown for its golden-yellow leaves and red spines on new shoots. A vigorous grower to 50'.

Salix (willow)
A large group of deciduous trees and shrubs, some of which grow well in seaside environments. *S. matsudana* 'Tortuosa' (corkscrew willow, dragon-claw willow) with twisted shoots and leaves, makes an interesting specimen tree. To 20'. It is tolerant of sandy soil and some salt spray and is drought resistant.

Sassafras albidum (sassafras)
Interesting native of coastal forests. Bright-green lobed and mitten-shaped leaves that turn bright orange and red in the autumn. 30–60'. Prefers full sun and ordinary soil and tolerates seaside conditions, including some salt spray. Drought resistant. Dried root bark is the source of sassafras teas.

Syringa reticulata (Japanese tree lilac)
Small tree valued for its cream-colored blossoms clusters in early summer. To 30'. Thrives in full sun and ordinary soil. Drought resistant once established. Some people dislike the fragrance of the blossoms, so plant away from house or outdoor living areas. 'Cameo Jewel' is a new variegated variety with yellow-cream foliage.

Tilia cordata (littleleaf linden)
Small, dark-green, heart-shaped leaves give tree an elegant look. Fragrant yellow flowers in late spring to early summer. To 60'. Thrives in full sun and ordinary soil. Drought resistant once established. Littleleaf linden takes pruning well and can be shaped or even trimmed as a hedge. 'Green Globe' and 'Lico' are dwarf varieties that look like lollipops on a stick. Check locally for new varieties that are appropriate for your area.

Lagerstroemia 'Natchez' (crape myrtle) has interesting bark that is smooth to the touch.

Sources

BOOKS ON SEASIDE GARDENING

Foley, Daniel J. *Gardening by the Sea from Coast to Coast*. Radnor, Pennsylvania: Chilton Book Company, 1965. An excellent book with a thorough plant list and useful information.

Menninger, Edwin A. *Seaside Plants of the World: A Guide to Planning, Planting and Maintaining Salt-Resistant Gardens*. New York: Hearthside Press, 1964. Primarily aimed at the gardener in Southern California and Florida, this book is difficult to find and to use but worthwhile for its list of 2,000 plants for seaside use, rated in terms of three "belts."

Murray, Steve. *A Guide to the Hereford Inlet Lighthouse Gardens with Tips and Observations for the Seaside Gardener*. North Wildwood, New Jersey: Hereford Inlet Lighthouse Commision, 2001. A great source for tips on dealing with the severe seaside environment.

Schmidt, R. Marilyn. *Gardening on the Eastern Seashore*. Chatsworth, New Jersey: Barnegat Light Press. The revised edition contains a useful list of 400 plants for East Coast gardeners. Available from Pine Barrens Press, P.O. Box 607, 3959 Route 563, Chatsworth, NJ 08019; (609) 894-4415.

SOURCES FOR PLANTS

There are hundreds of excellent sources for seaside plants. The following list provides a useful starting point.

Annual and perennial seeds

Park Seed Co., 1 Parkton Ave, Greenwood, SC 29647. (800) 213-0076. www.parkseed.com. An extensive variety of annual and perennial seeds. Catalogue: free.

Stokes Seeds, P.O. Box 548, Buffalo, NY 14240. (800) 396-9238. www.stokesseeds.com. A great selection of annual and perennial seeds. Catalogue: free.

Thompson & Morgan, Box 1308, Jackson, NJ 08527. (800) 274-7333. www.seeds.thompson-morgan.com/us. This house offers an extensive list of perennial and annual seeds. The free catalogue is extremely useful.

W. Atlee Burpee & Co., 300 Park Ave., Warminster, PA 18974. (800) 333-5808. www.burpee.com. Another house that offers a great variety of annual and perennial seeds. Catalogue: free.

Bulbs

Van Bourgondien, P.O. Box 2000, Virginia Beach, VA 23450. (800) 622-9959. www.dutchbulbs.com. A large selection of bulbs at reasonable prices. Catalogue: free.

Tropicals

Plant Delights Nursery, 9241 Sauls Rd. Raleigh, NC 27603. (919) 772-4794. www.plantdelights.com. Interesting perennials as well as native plants. Catalogue: free.

Rare Find Nursery, 957 Patterson Rd., Jackson, NJ 08527. (732) 833-0613. www.rarefindnursery.com. A great place to expand your horizons with unusual plants. Catalogue: $3 for 3 years.

Perennial plants and shrubs

Bluestone Perennials, 7211 Middle Ridge Rd., Madison, OH 44057. (800) 852-5243. www.bluestoneperennials.com. One of the best sources for perennials, shrubs, and more at very reasonable prices. Catalogue: free.

Wayside Gardens, 1 Garden Ln., Hodges, SC 29695. (800) 213-0379. www.waysidegardens.com. A stunning collection of perennials, bulbs, roses, shrubs, and trees. The free catalogue is extremely useful.

White Flower Farm, P.O. Box 50, Route 63, Litchfield, CT 06759. (800) 503-9624. www.whiteflowerfarm.com. A vast collection of perennials, bulbs, roses, shrubs, and trees. Catalogue: free.

Grasses

Earthly Pursuits, 2901 Kuntz Rd., Windsor Mill, MD 21244. (410) 496-2523. www.earthlypursuits.net. A broad selection of ornamental grasses, as well as bamboo and ferns.

Roses

Jackson & Perkins, 1 Rose Lane, Medford, OR 97501. (877) 322-2300. www.jacksonandperkins.com. America's largest purveyor of roses, also offering perennials and bulbs. Catalogue: free.

Roses of Yesterday and Today, 803 Brown's Valley Rd., Watsonville, CA 95076. (831) 728-1901. www.rosesofyesterday.com. This house offers a comprehensive selection of Old Garden roses and some difficult-to-find Modern roses. Catalogue: $5.00.

Water gardens

Lilypons Water Gardens, 6800 Lily Pons Rd., P.O. Box 10, Buckeystown, MD 21717. (800) 999-5459. www.lilypons.com. This firm provides everything you need to build a lily pond. Catalogue: free.

Index of Plant Names

189

192

Acknowledgments

We wish to thank so many people for their enthusiasm, encouragement, and cooperation while we were working on this book. In Maine, we are obliged to Gene Skewis Moll and her husband, Ed, for their kindness; Katie Dennis, for introducing us to so many gardeners in Northeast Harbor and Bar Harbor; and Mrs. Thomas Hall, Jane Robinson, George and Linda Smith, and the many gardeners who permitted us to enter and photograph their extraordinary gardens.

On the east end of Long Island, our neighbor and talented garden designer Judy Plant deserves special mention, as does designer Elizabeth Lear, for her kind enthusiasm and for introducing us to so many designers, architects, and homeowners in the area. Their efforts are well represented in these pages. We would also like to acknowledge Michael Graham of Deerfield; Frankenbach Nursery of Water Mill; designer Marla Gagnum, East Hampton, and Joanne Woodle, Peconic, Long Island; Ellen Kosciusko, Seton Shanley, Robert Dash, Emerick Bronson, Kate Tyree, Charles and Helga Michel, Harriet and Walter Weyer, Dr. Rutledge W. Howard of Boerne, Texas; Douglas E. Ward of Normandy Beach, New Jersey; Betsy Trundle of Virginia Beach, Virginia; and Tim Cottrell for their generous assistance. Thanks to Lito Denenburg for his support. We are grateful to Richard Iversen for his help on the tropical chapter and for sharing his glorious garden with us. We would also like to mention Steve Murray, who has done a magnificent job at Hereford Inlet Lighthouse Gardens in North Wildwood, New Jersey.

We are grateful to our editor, Eric Himmel, and his wife, Caroline, for inviting us to stay with them at their summer house on Fire Island and for introducing us to numerous gardeners in the area. Our thanks also to our literary agent, Rosalind Cole.

Finally, a special thanks to Tom Langhauser, whose keen eye and pre-dawn enthusiasm has enhanced the photographs.